P9-DYZ-939

MARISOL

AND OTHER PLAYS

MARISOL

AND OTHER PLAYS

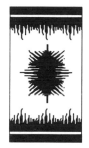

JOSÉ RIVERA

THEATRE COMMUNICATIONS GROUP

Marisol and Other Plays copyright © 1997 by José Rivera

Marisol copyright © 1992 by José Rivera
Each Day Dies with Sleep copyright © 1990 by José Rivera
Cloud Tectonics copyright © 1996 by José Rivera

Foreword copyright © 1997 by Tina Landau

Marisol and Other Plays is published by Theatre Communications Group, Inc.,
520 Eighth Ave., 24th Fl., New York, NY 10018-4156.

All rights reserved. Except for brief passages quoted in newspaper, magazine, radio or television reviews, no part of this book may be reproduced in any form or by any means, electronic or mechanical, including photocopying or recording, or by an information storage and retrieval system, without permission in writing from the publisher.

Professionals and amateurs are hereby warned that this material, being fully protected under the Copyright Laws of the United States of America and all other countries of the Berne and Universal Copyright Conventions, is subject to a royalty. All rights including, but not limited to, professional, amateur, recording, motion picture, recitation, lecturing, public reading, radio and television broadcasting, and the rights of translation into foreign languages are expressly reserved. Particular emphasis is placed on the question of readings and all uses of these plays by educational institutions, permission for which must be secured from the author's representative: Joyce Ketay, The Joyce Ketay Agency, 630 Ninth Ave., Suite 706, New York, NY 10036; (212) 354-6825.

On page v: Italo Calvino's quote is from *If on a winter's night a traveler*, English translation © 1981; translated by William Weaver; published by Harcourt Brace Jovanovich, Orlando, Florida. On page 70: Federico García Lorca's quote is from the poem "Landscape of a Pissing Multitude (Battery Place Nocturne)" in *Poet in New York* © 1988; edited by Christopher Maurer, translated by Greg Simon and Steven F. White; published by the Noonday Press, a Division of Farrar, Straus and Giroux, New York City. On page 133: Pablo Neruda's quote is from the poem "Juegas Todos Los Días . . ." in *Selected Poems* (Bilingual Edition) © 1970, edited by Nathaniel Tarn, translated by Anthony Kerrigan, W. S. Merwin, Alastair Reid and Nathaniel Tarn; published by Penguin Books, New York City. Julian Barnes's quote is from *A History of the World in 10½ Chapters* © 1989; published by Alfred A. Knopf, Inc., New York City; Mavis Gallant's quote is cited from the same source. Stephen W. Hawking's quote is from *A Brief History of Time* © 1988, published by Bantam, New York City. Danny Daniel's quote is from the song "Por El Amor De Una Mujer" by Los Panchos.

This publication is made possible in part with public funds from the New York State Council on the Arts, a State Agency.

TCG books are exclusively distributed to the book trade by Consortium Book Sales and Distribution, 1045 Westgate Dr., St. Paul, MN 55114.

Rivera, José.
Marisol and other plays / José Rivera. — 1st ed.
ISBN 1-55936-136-0
I. Title.
PS3568.I8294M37   1997
812'.54—dc21   97-5736
CIP

Cover photograph: "Untitled self portrait #12, 1989"
by Anne Arden McDonald. Courtesy of the Robin Rice Gallery, New York City.
Cover design, book design and composition by Lisa Govan

First Edition, June 1997
Fourth Printing, August 2007

For Heather, Adena and Teo

"I felt a kind of vertigo,
as if I were merely plunging
from one world to another,
and in each I arrived shortly
after the end of the world
had taken place."

—*Italo Calvino,*

IF ON A WINTER'S NIGHT A TRAVELER

CONTENTS

FOREWORD

by Tina Landau

My first encounter with José Rivera occurred 30,000 feet in the air, which perfectly sums up for me both the feeling of working on José's plays and the special world he invites us to inhabit. In the magical, mysterious Rivera-esque universe, we are somewhere else, somewhere related to the earth but not quite on it; we gaze out and see our little planet as if for the first time, against the sprawling backdrop of Nature, and see how tiny and ridiculous and beautiful it really is.

The airplane began its descent into Los Angeles. I was on my way to meet José for the first time, to discuss the possibility of my directing *Marisol* at the La Jolla Playhouse. I had just turned the last page of the script, and I will never forget the experience of looking down at a maze of freeways and swimming pools, a city which had recently been torn apart by race riots and fire. I saw the city as José does, from this unique view I now had: a glimpse of both heaven and hell, cloud and metal, the magic of the celestial and the odyssey of the earth-bound. L.A. suddenly looked different to me. Everything did.

A great writer does this: makes either the strange familiar or the familiar strange, as Brecht put it. José does both. Poised delicately between worlds, he writes of burning people and floating beds, of guardian angels and Nazi skinheads, of the storm of the century and candlelit dinners. And in the process, he asks us to see each two as one, and to see each anew.

"Magic realism." The term, applied loosely and often to José's work, causes him both great pride and frustration. "Magic realism" evolved in the shadows of dictatorship around the world, as a way of expressing the extraordinary events of history which seem to exceed the grasp of ordinary narrative. But this is not exactly how José has used it, or rather not exactly why he has developed his own personal rendition. What José shares with his great mentor and inspiration, Gabriel Garcia Marquez, is the notion that "transactions between the mundane and the extraordinary are not merely a literary technique, but a mirror of an intractable reality," as Michiko Kakutani has written. In José's view, what exists is not only the material world, but also the unseen world; the magical is part of the real.

José's theatre of imagination and poetry is also one of political and daily reality. His plays seem to start in hidden histories, inspired by something that actually happened, or someone he actually knew, or some image he actually saw: a man attacking people with a golf club on a New York City subway; a pregnant hitchhiker standing in the rain. José takes the stuff of real life and makes it *even more so*. In *Each Day Dies with Sleep*, as in real life, a family thrashes against the bonds of love and hate, only more so. In *Marisol*, as in real life, New York is on the verge of a breakdown, only more so. In *Cloud Tectonics*, as in real life, two people fall in love and time seems to stand still, only more so. In these extreme, hallucinatory worlds, the "more so" expresses a truth so bare, so big, that it can only be expressed in the metaphors José chooses. The worlds of José's plays are fantastical because they express the way things *really* are, under the surface. Each play contains its own complete play-world, a universe that functions with unique laws of time or space or behavior.

José's plays are not as much about individuals as they are about individuals in relation to the universe. The dialogue is not only between people but also between people and God, people and nature, people and the cosmos—and God (or Nature) has both a sense of humor and a temper. The moon has disappeared from the sky; the deluge has arrived; coffee is extinct. The individual is set against this panorama of a world gone wacko: a little figure struggling to stand upright, like Nelly, or to find a way to love, like Aníbal, or simply to survive, like Marisol. They try to remain human (Nelly wants to walk on two legs instead of four) or remember some lost self (Aníbal wants to speak Spanish). Marisol struggles to return to a semblance of humanity and embarks on a journey which, like the "hero path" in Joseph Campbell's view of mythology, leads her to her new role as hero. These characters struggle to keep their dignity, their passion and, often, their Puerto Rican-ness. In their search for what is lost, they become detectives and each play becomes a mystery, with the protagonist working to piece together a personal solution.

But none of José's plays are any *one* thing. The first time I read *Cloud*, I thought it was a suspense story: Who is Celestina? What are her secrets? The second time I read it, it was clearly a love story: What happens to time and space when two people fall in love? When I read the play for a third time, it became a philosophical discussion of the nature of Time itself: Is time something that can only be measured, or can it also be *felt*? How, exactly, is time relative? And then, one day it hit me: "Aha! the play is a comedy!" But that was mock revelation, because by that point I had realized the play was not *one* of these things *but all of them*.

While working on *Cloud*, José once asked me, "How do you study the clouds? How do you study Love?" Who knows—but I imagine it's a bit like trying to study or pin down José's plays: No matter how hard you try, the realities keep shifting, and you come face to face with the maddening, exhilarating truth that in many great things—like nature or love, sometimes a play—there is, at its heart, unfathomable mystery.

The hardest thing for me about directing these plays stems from this very multiplicity: How do you locate a tone, a style, create life in this odd, imbalanced place between the natural and the poetic? Just as Chekhov requires a certain approach from actors, or as Shakespeare or Beckett require other approaches to make their drama come alive, so does Rivera. Subtext functions in a certain way in one, thought in another, rhythm in a third . . .

I wish I could state here what the key to "Rivera" is. I know that it's important to follow the musical dictation, if you will, of José's italics, underlines and punctuation. I know that it's helpful to let each of the "lists" in his writing build, making each thing worse or bigger or better than the one before. I know that the environment needs to be treated as a character. I know that it all needs to be played with a light touch, that the humor and absurdity need to be embraced. I know, perhaps more than anything, that the actors need to believe in the reality of who they are and what they do and where they live. They cannot act the metaphor, or be the archetype. (If you are the Man With Scar Tissue, then you need to understand that your skin is literally burned off; or, if you are Johnny, you need to get inside what it feels like to have the jealous husbands of Los Angeles on your heels. You need to believe in the unbelievable.)

The continuing mystery of José's work compels me to keep doing it. I have a hunch, however, that I will never solve the mystery, because José's work doesn't stand still. Just as he taps into one explosive way to write a play, he is on to another.

Although on some level these three plays can be read as parts of each other—three beautiful, strong heroines, each continuing the others' journey—they also reveal a writer's strong urge to experiment, to evolve. For instance, these three plays can be read as investigations into the notion of Time on stage. José has said, "Each generation produces some kind of theatre revolutionary who handles an aspect of theatre in an original way." I think this is how José approaches Time. *Each Day* compresses it, proceeding at a frantic pace with scenes popping in and out of each other. *Marisol* elongates it, as the first act's episodes dissolve into a seamless second act, which seems to take place in eternal limbo. In *Cloud*, we are introduced to Celestina—for whom time is nothing and everything—and a world in which a quesadilla can be cooked in real time while forty years go by in an instant.

Here, then, is a theatre of ideas as well as a theatre of language, a theatre of images, a theatre with ambition and politics and heart. Here is a playwright who writes great roles for women. Here is a playwright who writes great roles for Puerto Ricans. Here is a playwright who, perhaps, as Nelly says about herself in *Each Day*, "grew up in the middle of the storm"—in this case, the storm of our collapsing urban centers—and yet has not forgotten that every time we cross the street safely we are blessed by an angel, and that every hitchhiker might be a Celestina for our cynical souls. Of the many, many things which José's plays are about for me, and of the many things I have learned from this thoughtful collaborator and friend, I would say it all comes down to something as simple—and complex—as Faith. Believing in what you can't see.

In José's plays, if something is remembered and uttered, then it can be kept alive. If Augie can remember and utter his daughter Nelly's name, the family will stay alive. If Anibal can remember and utter Spanish, his culture will stay alive . . . For me, the theatre is a vessel for our memories. In doing José's plays, we can remember—and utter a belief in mystery and magic and miracles.

Special thanks to Karina Arroyave, Tanya Berezin, Susan Berman, Robert Blacker, Ivonne Coll, Alex Colon, Chris Cunningham, Doris Difarnecio, Michael Dixon, Micha Espinosa, David Fenner, Max Ferra, Erica Gimpel, Cordelia Gonzalez, Michael Greif, Gregory Gunter, Michael Harris, V Craig Heidenreich, Adrienne Hiegel, Leslie Hope, Mame Hunt, Decater James, Morgan Jenness, Robert Jimenez, Jon Jory, Joyce Ketay, Susan Knight, Mark Lamos, Tina Landau, Roberta Levitow, Des McAnuff, Robert Montano, Javi Mulero, Carl Mulert, John Ortiz, Anne O'Sullivan, Robert A. Owens, Sharon Ott, Luis Antonio Ramos, Carlos Ramos, Camilia Sanes, Tim Sanford, Amy Scholl, Esther Scott, Phyllis Somerville, Marcus Stern, Charlie Stratton, Skipp Sudduth, Joseph Urla, Danitra Vance, Randy Vasquez and Michele Volansky.

MARISOL

Marisol was originally commissioned and developed by INTAR Hispanic Arts Center (Max Ferra, Artistic Director) through a grant from the Rockefeller Foundation.

The play received its world premiere at the 1992 Annual Humana Festival of New American Plays at the Actors Theatre of Louisville (Jon Jory, Producing Director), in Louisville, Kentucky, on March 13, 1992. It was directed by Marcus Stern; the set design was by Paul Owen; the costume design was by Laura A. Patterson; the lighting design was by Mary Louise Geiger; the sound design was by Darron West; and the stage manager was James Mountcastle. The cast was as follows:

ANGEL	Esther Scott
MARISOL	Karina Arroyave
MAN WITH GOLF CLUB,	
MAN WITH ICE CREAM,	
LENNY,	
MAN WITH SCAR TISSUE	V Craig Heidenreich
JUNE	Susan Knight
HOMELESS PERSON	Carlos Ramos

Marisol was produced by the New York Shakespeare Festival (George C. Wolfe, Producer), in association with the Hartford Stage Company (Mark Lamos, Artistic Director), in New York City in May 1993. It was directed by Michael Greif; the set design was by Debra Booth; the costume design was by Angela Wendt; the lighting design was by Kenneth Posner; the sound design was by David Budries; the violence director was David Leong; the original music was by Jill Jaffe; and the production stage manager was Lori M. Doyle. The cast was as follows:

ANGEL	Danitra Vance
MARISOL	Cordelia González
YOUNG WOMAN	Doris Difarnecio
MAN WITH GOLF CLUB,	
MAN WITH ICE CREAM,	
LENNY,	
MAN WITH SCAR TISSUE	Skipp Sudduth
JUNE	Anne O'Sullivan
WOMAN WITH FURS,	
RADIO ANNOUNCER	Phyllis Somerville
VOICES, HOMELESS PEOPLE	Doris Difarnecio,
	Decater James,
	Robert Jimenez,
	Anne O'Sullivan,
	Phyllis Somerville
GUITARIST	Chris Cunningham

CHARACTERS

ANGEL

MARISOL

MAN WITH GOLF CLUB ⎤

MAN WITH ICE CREAM ⎥ *All can be*
played by the
LENNY ⎥ *same actor*

MAN WITH SCAR TISSUE ⎦

JUNE

WOMAN WITH FURS

RADIO ANNOUNCER

HOMELESS PEOPLE

PLACE

New York City.

TIME

The present.

ACT ONE

———————————

Scene One

New York City. The present.

Lights up on an upstage brick wall running the width of the stage and going as high as the theatre will allow. The windows in the wall are shielded by iron security gates. The highest windows are boarded up.

Spray-painted on the wall is this graffiti-poem:

The moon carries the souls of dead people to heaven.
The new moon is dark and empty.
It fills up every month
with new glowing souls
then it carries its silent burden to God. WAKE UP.

The "WAKE UP" looks like it was added to the poem by someone else.

Downstage of the wall is a tall ladder coming down at an angle. Sitting on the ladder is Marisol's Guardian Angel.

The Angel is a young black woman in ripped jeans, sneakers, and black T-shirt. Crude silver wings hang limply from the back of the Angel's diamond-studded black leather jacket. Though she radiates tremendous heat and light, there's something tired and

5

lonely about the Angel: she looks like an urban warrior, a suffering burnt-out soldier of some lost cause. She watches the scene below with intense concern.

Floating in the sky is a small gold crown inside a clear glass box.

Lights up on the subway car: a filth-covered bench.

It's late night. Late winter.

Marisol Perez, an attractive Puerto Rican woman of twenty-six, sits in the subway car. Marisol has dark hair and deep, smart, dark eyes. She is a young urban professional: smartly dressed, reading the New York Times, *returning to her Bronx apartment after a long day at her Manhattan job. She wears heavy winter clothing. She has no idea she's being watched by an angel.*

SUBWAY ANNOUNCER: . . . and a pleasant evening to all the ladies. 180th Street will be the next and last stop. Step lively, guard your valuables, trust no one.

(The Man With Golf Club enters the subway car. He's a young white man, twenties, in a filthy black T-shirt and ripped jeans; his long matted hair hangs over blazing eyes. His shoes are rags and his mind is shot. The man looks at Marisol and "shoots" the club like an Uzi.

Marisol has taught herself not to show fear or curiosity on the subway. She digs deeper into her paper. The Man talks to Marisol.)

GOLF CLUB: It was the shock that got me. I was so shocked all I could see was pain all around me: little spinning starlights of pain 'cause of the shocking thing the angel just told me.

(He waits for a reaction. Marisol refuses to look at him.)

You see, she was always *there* for me. I could *count* on her. She was my very own god-blessed little angel! My own gift from God!

(No response. He makes a move toward Marisol. She looks at him, quickly sizing him up . . .)

MARISOL: God help you, you get in my face.

GOLF CLUB: But last night she crawled into the box I occupy on 180th Street in the Bronx. I was sleeping: nothing special walking through my thoughts 'cept the usual panic over my empty stomach, and the windchill factor, and how, oh *how*, was I *ever* gonna replace my lost Citibank MasterCard?

MARISOL: I have no money.

(Marisol tries to slide away from the Man, trying to show no fear. He follows.)

GOLF CLUB: She folded her hot silver angelwings under her leather jacket and creeped into my box last night, reordering the air, waking me up with the shock, the bad news that she was gonna *leave me forever* . . .

MARISOL *(Getting freaked)*: Man, why don't you just get a job?!

GOLF CLUB: *Don't you see?* She once stopped Nazi skinheads from setting me on fire in Van Cortlandt Park! Do you get it now, lady?! I live on the street! I am dead meat without my guardian angel! I'm gonna be *food* . . . a fucking *appetizer* for all the Hitler youth and their cans of *gasoline* . . .

(The Man lunges at Marisol and rips the newspaper from her. She's on her feet, ready for a fight.)

MARISOL *(To God)*: Okay, God! Kill him now! Take him out!

GOLF CLUB *(Truly worried)*: That means you don't have any protection either. Your guardian angel is gonna leave you too. That means, in the next *four or five seconds*, I could change the entire course of your life . . .

MARISOL *(To God)*: Blast him into little bits! Turn him into salt!

GOLF CLUB *(Calm, almost pitying)*: I could turn you into one of me. I could fix it so every time you look in the mirror . . . every time you dream . . . or close your eyes in some hope

less logic that closed eyes are a shield against nightmares . . .
you're gonna think you turned into me . . .

*(The Man makes a move toward Marisol. The Angel reacts.
There's an earsplitting scream as the subway stops. Marisol and
the Man are thrown violently across the subway car. The Man
falls. Marisol seizes her chance, pushes the disoriented Man
away, and runs out of the subway car into the street. Lights to
black on the subway. The Man exits in the dark.)*

Scene Two

*Lights up on the street: a small empty space with a battered city
trash can. It's snowing lightly. The shivering Marisol stops to look
up at the sky. She crosses herself.*

MARISOL: Thank you.

*(No response from the Angel. It stops snowing as Marisol leaves
the street and enters:)*

Scene Three

*Lights up on Marisol's apartment: bed, table, lamp, clock, off-
stage bathroom, and large romanticized picture of a traditional
Catholic guardian angel on the wall.*
   *Marisol quickly runs in, slamming and locking the door
behind her. She runs to the window to make sure the security
gates are locked.*
   *She tries to catch her breath. She takes off her coat. She notices
an army of cockroaches on the floor. She stomps them angrily until
every last one is dead. This seems to make her feel a little better.*
   *She collapses into bed. She pounds her pillow angrily.
Exhausted, she checks a knife she keeps under her pillow. She puts
it back and lies on her bed, trying to calm herself and just
breathe.*

As she changes her clothes she fixes herself a drink and downs it.
She checks the crucifix, horseshoe, rabbit's foot, prayer cards,
milagros, *medicine bundles, statuettes of Buddha and other good-*
luck charms kept under the bed. She crosses herself and closes her
eyes.

MARISOL: Matthew, Mark, Luke and John.
Bless the bed that I lie on.
Four corners to my bed.
Four angels 'round my head.
One to watch and one to pray.
And two to bear my soul away.

(Marisol crosses herself, opens her eyes and lies down. Then the
noises begin. They come at Marisol from apartments all around
her. Doors are slammed, bottles smashed, radiator pipes pounded,
stereos played loud. Then the voices join in.)

VOICE #1 *(Female)*: Ave Maria purisima, donde esta el heat?

(Marisol sits up. She can't believe this bullshit is starting
again . . .)

VOICE #2 *(Female, a high-decibel shriek)*: Matthew? It's Sandy! I
KNOW YOU'RE IN THERE. STOP HIDING FROM
ME, YOU MALIGNANT FUCK!

(Marisol starts rubbing her pounding head.)

VOICE #3 *(Male)*: Ah yeah yeah man you gotta help me man they
broke my fuckin' *head* open . . .

(Marisol runs to her window, shakes the iron gates.)

MARISOL: *Mira,* people are trying to sleep!
VOICE #2: YOU'RE PISSING ME OFF, MATTHEW, OPEN
THE DOOR!
VOICE #1: *Donde esta el* heat?? *NO TENGO* HEAT, *coño!*

VOICE #2: MATTHEEEEEEEEEEEEEEEEW!

(Marisol dives back into bed, covering her head, trying not to hear. The noises increase and the voices come faster, louder, overlapping . . .)

VOICE #3: . . . I was jus' tryin' to sell 'em some dope man . . .
VOICE #2: MATTHEW, GODDAMMIT, IT'S SANDY! SANDY! YOUR *GIRLFRIEND*, YOU WITLESS *COCK*!
VOICE #1: *Me vas a matar* without *el* fucking heat!!
VOICE #2: MATTHEEEEEEEEWWWWWWW! OPEN THIS DOOOOOOOOOOOOR!
VOICE #3: . . . so they hadda go bust my fuckin' head open oh look haha there go my busted brains floppin' 'round the floor I'm gonna step right on 'em I'm not careful man I shouldda got their fuckin' *badge* numbers . . .

(Marisol bangs on the floor with a shoe.)

MARISOL: Some people work in the morning!!
VOICE #3: . . . think I'll pick up my brains right now man get a shovel 'n' scoop up my soakin' brainbag off this messy linoleum floor man sponge up my absentee motherfuckin' *mind* . . .
VOICE #2: THAT'S IT, MATTHEW! YOU'RE DEAD. I'M COMING BACK WITH A GUN AND I'M GONNA KILL YOU AND THEN I'M GONNA KILL EVERYONE IN THIS APARTMENT BUILDING INCLUDING THE CHILDREN!

(The voices stop. Marisol waits. Thinking it's over, Marisol gets into bed and tries to sleep. Beat. Marisol starts to nod off. There's suddenly furious knocking at Marisol's door.)

VOICE #2: MATTHEW! I'M BACK! I'VE GOT MY DADDY'S GUN! AND YOU'RE GONNA DIE RIGHT NOW!

(Marisol runs to the door.)

MARISOL: Matthew doesn't live here! You have the wrong apartment!

VOICE #2: Matthew, *who's that*???

MARISOL: Matthew lives next door!!

VOICE #2: IS THAT YOUR NEW GIRLFRIEND, MATTHEW???! OH YOU'RE DEAD. YOU'RE REALLY DEAD NOW!!

(A gun is cocked. Marisol dives for cover. The Angel reacts. Suddenly, the stage is blasted with white light.

There's complete silence: the rattling, banging, screaming all stop. We hear crickets.

Marisol, amazed by the instant calm, goes to the door, looks through the peephole. She cautiously opens the door.

There's a small pile of salt on the floor. At first, Marisol just looks at it, too amazed to move. Then she bends down to touch the salt, letting it run through her fingers.)

MARISOL: Salt?

(Frightened, not sure she knows what this means, Marisol quickly closes and locks the door. She gets into bed and turns out the light. Lights down everywhere except on the Angel.)

Scene Four

Lights shift in Marisol's apartment as the Angel climbs down the ladder to Marisol's bed.

Marisol feels the tremendous heat given off by the Angel. The Angel backs away from Marisol so as not to burn her. The Angel goes to the window and looks out. Her voice is slightly amplified. She speaks directly to Marisol, who sleeps.

Throughout the scene, the light coming in through Marisol's window goes up slowly, until, by the end, it's the next morning.

ANGEL: A man is worshiping a fire hydrant on Taylor Avenue, Marisol. He's draping rosaries on it, genuflecting hard. An old woman's selling charmed chicken blood in see-through

Ziplock bags for a buck. They're setting another homeless man on fire in Van Cortlandt Park.

(The Angel rattles the metal gate.)

Cut that shit out you fucking Nazis!

(The Angel goes to Marisol's door and checks the lock. She stomps cockroaches. She straightens up a little.)

I swear, best thing that could happen to this city is immediate evacuation followed by fire on a massive scale. Melt it all down. Consume the ruins. Then put the ashes of those evaporated dreams into a big urn and sit the urn on the desks of a few thousand oily politicians. Let them smell the disaster like we do.

(The Angel goes to Marisol's bed and looks at her. Marisol's heart beats faster and she starts to hyperventilate.)

So what do you believe in, Marisol? You believe in me? Or do you believe your senses? If so, what's that taste in your mouth?

(The Angel clicks her fingers. Although Marisol responds, she remains sleeping throughout the following scene.)

MARISOL *(Tasting)*: Oh my God, *arroz con gandules*! Yum!
ANGEL: What's your favorite smell, Marisol?

(Click!)

MARISOL *(Sniffing)*: The ocean! I smell the ocean!
ANGEL: Do you like sex, Marisol?

(Click! Marisol is seized by powerful sexual spasms that wrack her body and nearly throw her off the bed. When they end, Marisol stretches out luxuriously: exhausted but happy.)

MARISOL *(Laughing)*: I've got this wild energy running through my body!

(The Angel gets closer to her.)

ANGEL: Here's your big chance, baby. What would you like to ask the Angel of the Lord?

MARISOL *(Energized)*: Are you real? Are you true? Are you gonna make the Bronx safe for me? Are you gonna make miracles and reduce my rent? Is it true angels' favorite food is Thousand Island dressing? Is it true your shit smells like mangoes and when you're drunk you speak Portuguese?!

ANGEL: Honey, last time *I* was drunk . . .

(Marisol gets a sudden, horrifying realization.)

MARISOL: *Wait a minute—am I dead?* Did I die tonight? How did I miss that? Was it the man with the golf club? Did he beat me to death? Oh my God. I've been dead all night. And when I look around I see that Death is my ugly apartment in the Bronx. No this can't be Death! Death can't have this kind of furniture!

ANGEL: God, you're so cute, I could eat you up. No. You're still alive.

(Marisol is momentarily relieved—then she suddenly starts touching her stomach as she gets a wild, exhilarating idea:)

MARISOL: *Am I pregnant with the Lord's baby?!* Is the new Messiah swimming in my electrified womb? Is the supersperm of God growing a mythic flower deep in the secret greenhouse inside me? Will my morning sickness taste like communion wine? This is amazing—*billions* of women on earth, and I get knocked up by God!

ANGEL: No baby, no baby, no baby, no baby—No. Baby.

(Beat. Marisol is a little disappointed.)

MARISOL: No? Then what is it? Are you real or not? 'Cause if you're real and God is real and the Gospels are real, this would be the perfect time to tell me. 'Cause I once looked for angels, I did, in every shadow of my childhood—but I never found any. I thought I'd find you hiding inside the notes I sang to myself as a kid. The songs that put me to sleep and kept me from killing myself with fear. But I didn't see you then.

(The Angel doesn't answer. Her silence—her very presence— starts to unhinge Marisol.)

C'mon! Somebody up there has to tell me why I live the way I do! What's going *on* here, anyway? Why is there a war on children in this city? Why are apples extinct? Why are they planning to drop human insecticide on overpopulated areas of the Bronx? Why has the color blue disappeared from the sky? Why does common rainwater turn your skin bright red? Why do cows give salty milk? Why did the Plague kill half my friends? AND WHAT HAPPENED TO THE MOON? Where did the moon go? How come nobody's seen it in nearly *nine months . . . ?*

(Marisol is trying desperately to keep from crying. The Angel gets into bed with Marisol. Contact with the Angel makes Marisol gasp. She opens her mouth to scream, but nothing comes out. Marisol collapses—her whole body goes limp.
Marisol rests her head on the Angel's lap. Electricity surges gently through Marisol's body. She is feeling no pain, fear, or loneliness. The Angel strokes her hair.)

ANGEL: I kick-started your heart, Marisol. I wired your nervous system. I pushed your fetal blood in the right direction and turned the foam in your infant lungs to oxygen. When you were six and your parents were fighting, I helped you pretend you were underwater: that you were a cold-blooded fish, in the bottom of the black ocean, far away and safe. When racists ran you out of school at ten, screaming . . .

MARISOL: . . . "kill the spik" . . .

ANGEL: . . . I turned the monsters into little columns of salt! At last count, one plane crash, one collapsed elevator, one massacre at the hands of a right-wing fanatic with an Uzi, and sixty-six-thousand-six-hundred-and-three separate sexual assaults never happened because of me.

MARISOL: Wow. Now I don't have to be so paranoid . . . ?

(The Angel suddenly gets out of bed. Marisol curls up in a fetal position. The Angel is nervous now, full of hostile energy, anxious.)

ANGEL: Now the bad news.

(The Angel goes to the window. She's silent a moment as she contemplates the devastated Bronx landscape.)

MARISOL *(Worried)*: What?

(The Angel finds it very hard to tell Marisol what's on her mind.)

ANGEL: I can't expect you to understand the political ins and outs of what's going on. But you have eyes. You asked me questions about children and water and war and the moon: the same questions I've been asking myself for a thousand years.

(We hear distant explosions. Marisol's body responds with a jolt.)

MARISOL *(Quiet)*: What's that noise?

ANGEL: The universal body is sick, Marisol. Constellations are wasting away, the nauseous stars are full of blisters and sores, the infected earth is running a temperature, and everywhere the universal mind is wracked with amnesia, boredom, and neurotic obsessions.

MARISOL *(Frightened)*: Why?

ANGEL: Because God is old and dying and taking the rest of us with Him. And for too long, much too long, I've been looking the other way. Trying to stop the massive hemorrhage with my little hands. With my prayers. But it didn't work and I knew if I didn't do something soon, it would be too late.

MARISOL *(Frightened)*: What did you do?

ANGEL: I called a meeting. And I urged the Heavenly Hierarchies—the Seraphim, Cherubim, Thrones, Dominions, Principalities, Powers, Virtues, Archangels and Angels—to vote to stop the universal ruin . . . by slaughtering our senile God. And they did. Listen well, Marisol: angels are going to kill the King of Heaven and restore the vitality of the universe with His blood. And I'm going to lead them.

(Marisol takes this in silently—then suddenly erupts—her body shaking with fear and energy.)

MARISOL: Okay, I wanna wake up now!

ANGEL: There's going to be war. A revolution of angels.

MARISOL: GOD IS GREAT! GOD IS GOOD! THANK YOU FOR OUR NEIGHBORHOOD!

ANGEL: Soon we're going to send out spies, draft able-bodied celestial beings, raise taxes . . .

MARISOL: THANK YOU FOR THE BIRDS THAT SING! THANK YOU GOD FOR EVERYTHING!

ANGEL: Soon we're going to take off our wings of peace, Marisol, and put on our wings of war. Then we're going to spread blood and vigor across the sky and reawaken the dwindling stars!

MARISOL *(Reciting fast)*: "And there was war in Heaven; Michael and his angels fought against the dragon; and the dragon fought—"

ANGEL: It could be suicide. A massacre. He's better armed. Better organized. And, well, a little omniscient. But we *have* to win. *(Beat)* And when we do win . . . when we crown the new God, and begin the new millennium . . . the earth will be restored. The moon will return. The degradation of the animal kingdom will end. Men and women will be elevated to a higher order. All children will speak Latin. And Creation will finally be perfect.

(Distant thunder and lightning. The Angel quickly goes to the window to read the message in the lightning. She turns to Marisol, who is struggling to wake up.)

It also means I have to leave you. I can't stay. I can't protect you anymore.

(Beat.)

MARISOL: What? You're *leaving* me?
ANGEL: I don't want to. I love you. I thought you had to know. But now I have to go and fight—
MARISOL: I'm going to be alone?
ANGEL: And that's what you have to do, Marisol. You have to fight. You can't *endure* anymore. You can't trust luck or prayer or mercy or other people. When I drop my wings, all hell's going to break loose and soon you're not going to recognize the world—so get yourself some *power*, Marisol, whatever you do.
MARISOL: What's going to happen to me without you . . . ?

(The Angel goes to Marisol and tries to kiss her.)

ANGEL: I don't know.

(Marisol lashes out, trying to hit the Angel. Marisol spits at the Angel. The Angel grabs Marisol's hands.)

MARISOL: *I'm gonna be meat!* I'M GONNA BE FOOD!!

(By now the lights are nearly up full: it's the next morning. The Angel holds the struggling Marisol.)

ANGEL: Unless you want to join us—
MARISOL: NOOOOO!!

(Marisol fights. Her alarm clock goes off.

The Angel lets Marisol go and climbs up the ladder and disappears.

Marisol wakes up violently—she looks around in a panic—instantly goes for the knife under her pillow.

It takes her a few moments to realize she's home in her bed.

She puts the knife away. Turns off the alarm clock. She thinks: "I must have been dreaming." She shakes her head, catches her breath and tries to calm down. She wipes the sweat from her face.

Marisol gets out of bed. She goes to the window and looks down at the street—her eyes filled with new terror. She runs to her offstage bathroom.)

Scene Five

Lights up on Marisol's office in Manhattan: two metal desks facing each other covered in books and papers. One desk has a small radio.

June enters the office. She's an Irish-American, thirty-six: bright, edgy, hyper, dressed in cool East Village clothes. Her wild red hair and all-American freckles provide a vivid contrast to Marisol's Latin darkness. June tries to read the New York Post *but she can't concentrate. She keeps waiting for Marisol to appear. June turns on the radio.*

RADIO VOICE: . . . sources indicate the president's psychics believe they know where the moon has gone to. They claim to see the moon hovering over the orbit of Saturn, looking lost. Pentagon officials are considering plans to spend billions on a space tug to haul the moon back to earth. The tug would attach a long chain to the moon so it never strays from its beloved earth again. One insider has been quoted as saying the White House hopes to raise revenues for Operation Moon Rescue by taxing lunatics. Responding to allegations that cows are giving salty milk because grass is contaminated, government scientists are drafting plans to develop a new strain of cow that lives by eating Astroturf.

(June turns off the radio. Marisol enters the office in a change of clothes. June sees her and lets out a yell of joy. She goes to Marisol and embraces her.)

JUNE: Marisol! Thank God! I couldn't sleep all night because of you!

(Marisol, still shaken by the night's strange visions, is dazed, unhappy. She pulls away from June.)

MARISOL *(Wary)*: What's the matter?

JUNE *(Grabbing her)*: You died! You died! It was all over the networks last night! You're on the front page of the *Post*!

(June shows Marisol the paper. On the cover is a closeup of a young woman's battered corpse. June reads:)

"*Twenty-six*-year-old *Marisol Perez* of 180th Street in the Bronx was bludgeoned to death on the IRT Number Two last night. The attack occurred 11:00 P.M."

(Marisol tries to remain calm as she looks at the hideous picture.)

I thought it was you. And I tried to call you last night but do you have any idea how many Marisol Perezes there are in the Bronx phone book? Only seven pages. I couldn't sleep.

MARISOL *(Barely calm)*: How did he kill her?

JUNE: Fucking barbarian beat her with a *golf club*, can you believe that? Like a caveman kills its *dinner*, fucking freak. I'm still upset.

(Marisol, numb, gives the paper back to June.)

MARISOL: It wasn't me, June.

JUNE: It could have been you, living alone in that marginal neighborhood, all the chances you take. Like doesn't this scare you? Isn't it past time to leave the Bronx behind?

(Marisol looks at June fully for the first time, trying to focus her thoughts.)

MARISOL: But it wasn't me. I didn't die last night.

(Marisol sits at her desk. June looks at the paper.)

JUNE *(Not listening)*: Goddamn vultures are having a field day with this, vast close-ups of Marisol Perez's pummeled face on TV, I mean what's the *point*? There's a prevailing sickness out there, I'm telling you, the Dark Ages are here, Visigoths are climbing the city walls, and I've never felt more like raw food in my life. Am I upsetting you with this?

(Marisol rubs her throbbing head.)

MARISOL: Yeah.
JUNE: Good. Put the fear of God in you. Don't let them catch you not ready, okay? You gotta be prepared to really *fight* now!
MARISOL *(Looks at her, surprised)*: Why do you say that? Did somebody tell you to say that?

(June gives Marisol a long look.)

JUNE: Something wrong with you today? You look like shit. You, Miss Puerto Rican Yuppy Princess of the Universe, you never look like shit.

(Marisol tries to smile, to shake off her fear.)

MARISOL: It's nothing. Let's get to work. If I don't get this manuscript off my desk . . .

(Marisol opens up a manuscript and tries to read it. June closes the manuscript.)

JUNE: Something happen to you last night?

MARISOL: No—it's—nothing—it's—*my body*—it feels like. Like it fits into my clothes all wrong today. Every person on the subway this morning gave me the shivers. They all looked so hungry. I keep hearing children crying. I keep smelling burnt flesh. And now there's a woman with my exact name killed on my exact street last night. *(Beat)* And I had this dream. A winged woman. A black angel with beautiful wings. She came to my bed and said she loved me.

JUNE *(Very interested)*: Oh?

MARISOL: She seemed so real. So absolute. Virtuous and powerful, incapable of lying, exalted, sublime, radiant, pure, perfect, fulgent.

JUNE: Fulgent?

(June takes Marisol by the shoulders and looks in her eyes.)

Whoa! Marisol! Yo! That didn't happen. You dreamed it. It's Roman Catholic bullshit.

MARISOL: . . . now I feel sorry. I just feel so sorry for everything . . .

(Marisol goes downstage and looks up at the sky, expecting to see something but not knowing what. She's fighting tears. June looks at her: Marisol's definitely not herself today.
June goes to her, embraces her. Marisol holds June for dear life. June tries to cheer Marisol up.)

JUNE: Lookit, I think your dream is like the moon's disappearance. It's all a lot of premillennium jitters. I've never seen so much nervousness. It's still up there but paranoia has clouded our view. That shit can happen you know.

(Marisol pulls away from June.)

MARISOL: I don't think the moon's disappearance is psychological. It's like the universe is senile, June. Like we're at the part of history where everything breaks down. Do you smell smoke?

(The lights begin to subtly go down. June notices the darkness right away. She looks at her watch.)

JUNE: Wait! It's nine-thirty! They're expecting the smoke from that massive fire in Ohio to reach New York by nine-thirty.

(June and Marisol look out the window. The lights go darker and darker.)

Jesus! Those are a million trees burning!

(June and Marisol calmly watch the spectacle.)

Christ, you can smell the polyester . . . the burnt malls . . . the defaulted loans . . . the unemployment . . . the flat vowels . . .

(Lights begin to go up. Marisol and June stand at the window and watch the black smoke begin to drift toward Europe. Silence. They look at each other. The whole thing suddenly strikes them as absurd—they laugh.)

Fuck it, I'm going on break. You want something from downstairs? Coffee? I'm going for coffee.

MARISOL: Coffee's extinct, June.

JUNE *(She hates tea)*: Tea—I meant *tea*. I'll get us both a cup of tea, try to carry on like normal. I swear, one more natural cataclysm like that and I'm going home. Are you okay?

(Marisol nods yes. June leaves the office. Marisol quickly starts reading from her manuscript.)

MARISOL *(With growing surprise)*: ". . . Salt is in the food and mythology of cultures old and new. Ancient writers believed that angels in heaven turned into salt when they died. Popular mythology holds that during the Fall of Satan, angels who were killed in battle fell into the primordial ocean, which was then fresh water. Today, the oceans are salted by the decomposed bodies of fallen angels . . ."

(The Man With Ice Cream enters the office.

He wears a business suit and licks an ice cream cone.
He smiles at Marisol, who looks at him, instantly sensing
trouble.)

ICE CREAM: I was in the movie *Taxi Driver* with Robert De Niro
and the son-of-a-gun never paid me.

MARISOL: Uhm. Are you looking for someone?

ICE CREAM: The Second A.D. said this is where I go to collect my
pay for my work in *Taxi Driver.*

MARISOL: This isn't a film company, sir. We publish science
books. I think there's a film company on the tenth floor.

ICE CREAM: No, this is the place. I'm sure this is the place.

MARISOL: Well . . . you know, sir . . . maybe if I called security for
you . . .

ICE CREAM: I worked real hard on that picture. It was my big
break. And of course, working with a genius like De Niro is
like Actor Heaven, but, c'mon, I still need the money!

MARISOL: I'm a busy woman, sir, I have a department to run—

ICE CREAM: I mean, I don't want to get temperamental, but *Taxi
Driver* came out a long time ago and I still haven't been paid!

MARISOL: Yeah, I'll call security for you—

ICE CREAM *(In despair)*: Christ, I have bills! I have rent! I have a
toddler in a Catholic preschool! I have an agent screaming
for his ten percent! *And how the fuck am I supposed to pay for
this ice cream cone? Do you think ice cream is free? Do you think
Carvel gives this shit out for nothing?*

MARISOL *(Calling out)*: June?! Is somebody on this floor?!

ICE CREAM: Don't fuck with me, lady. I once played a Nazi skinhead in a TV movie-of-the-week. I once set a man on fire in
Van Cortlandt Park for CBS! *And I really liked that role!*

(The Man throws the ice cream into Marisol's face. June runs on.)

JUNE: LEAVE HER ALONE YOU SCUMBAG!

*(June hits the Man as hard as she can. She pummels him. He
howls like a dog and runs out of the office. June runs after him.
Off:)*

SOMEBODY HELP ME GET HIM!

(As Marisol wipes the ice cream from her face, we hear footsteps going into the distance. Then footsteps returning. June runs back in, panting.)

He's gone. *(She picks up the phone)* Security? *YOU FUCK-ING BOZOS! WHY DON'T YOU DO YOUR JOB AND STOP LETTING MANIACS INTO THE BUILDING?!*

(June slams down the phone. She goes to Marisol, who is still wiping ice cream from her clothes. She's trembling.)

MARISOL: Vanilla almond. I'll never be able to eat vanilla almond again.

JUNE: Okay, that's IT, you and I are taking the rest of the day off, going to my house where it's *safe, fuck* everybody, I've had it with this death trap . . .

(June starts to hustle Marisol out of the office.
Marisol looks up—she's frozen by a vision.
Lights up, far above Marisol. The Angel is there, cleaning an Uzi submachine gun, humming quietly. Marisol isn't sure she's really seeing what she's seeing.
June looks up, sees nothing, and pulls Marisol offstage. Lights down on the Angel, who disappears in the dark.)

Scene Six

Lights up on June's apartment: a marbleized Formica table and matching red chairs.
It's later that day. June and Marisol enter. June automatically stomps cockroaches as she enters.

JUNE: . . . so we agitated for them to install metal detectors in all the buildings on this block. That'll definitely cut down on the random homicides.

MARISOL: That's civilized.

JUNE *(Brightly)*: That's Brooklyn.

MARISOL: What's that huge ugly windowless building with the smokestacks and armed guards across the street?

JUNE: Me? I think it's where they bring overthrown brutal right-wing dictators from Latin America to live, 'cause a friend's a friend, right?

MARISOL: I really appreciate this, June.

JUNE: Good, 'cause now I have to issue you a warning about my fucked-up brother who lives with me.

MARISOL: You do?

JUNE: Uhm. Lenny's a little weird about women. His imagination? It takes off on him on the slightest provocation and, uh, he doesn't know, you know, a reasonable way to channel his turbulent sexual death fantasies . . .

MARISOL: This is a long warning, June.

JUNE: He knows about you. Shit I've told him for two years. And so he's developed this *thing* for you, like he draws *pictures* of you, in crayon, covering every inch of his bedroom. He's thirty-four, you know, but he has the mental capacity of a child.

(Lenny enters. Lenny has uncontrollable hair that makes him look a little crazy. He can stand very, very still for a very long time. He goes immediately to the window without looking at June or Marisol.)

LENNY *(Indicating window)*: Wrong. It's a federally funded torture center where they violate people who have gone over their credit card limit.

JUNE *(Wary)*: Marisol, this is Lenny, the heat-seeking device. Lenny, this is Marisol Perez and you're *wrong*.

LENNY *(At window)*: I've seen them bring the vans, June. So shut up. People tied up. Guards with truncheons. Big fat New York City police with dogs. It happens late at night. But you can hear the screams. They cremate the bodies. That's why Brooklyn smells so funny.

MARISOL *(Nervous)*: I owe a lot of money to the MasterCard people.

(Lenny suddenly turns to Marisol. He is utterly focused on her.)

JUNE *(To Marisol)*: What he says is not proven.

LENNY: *Everybody* knows, June. It's a political *issue*. If you weren't so right wing—

JUNE: I am not right wing, you punk, don't EVER call me that! I happen to be the last true practicing communist in New York!

(Lenny keeps staring at Marisol.)

LENNY: You were on the news. You died on the news. But that was a different one.

MARISOL: She and I have the same name. Had.

LENNY *(Approaching Marisol)*: I'm so glad you didn't die before I got a chance to meet you.

(Lenny suddenly takes Marisol's hand and kisses it. June tries to step in between them.)

JUNE: That's enough, Lenny—I didn't bring her here to feed on . . .

LENNY *(Holding Marisol's hand)*: I went to your neighborhood this morning. To see the kind of street that would kill a Marisol Perez. I walked through Van Cortlandt Park. I played in the winter sunlight, watched perverts fondling snowmen, and at high noon, the dizziest time of the day, I saw a poor homeless guy being set on fire by Nazi skinheads—

JUNE: That's *it*, Lenny.

(June pulls Lenny aside. He knows he's in for a lecture.)

LENNY: What?

JUNE: We had a hard day. We came here to relax. So take a deep breath—

LENNY: She talked to me first—

JUNE: Listen to me before you say anything more. Are you listening?

LENNY: *Yes. Okay.*

JUNE: Let's cool our hormones, okay? Before the psychodrama starts in earnest?

LENNY: Yes. All right.

JUNE: Are we really?

(Lenny pulls away from June.)

LENNY *(To Marisol)*: Hey, honey, you wanna see my sculpture?

(Lenny runs to his offstage bedroom before Marisol can reply. June grabs her coat angrily.)

JUNE: You wanna get outta here? He's raving.

LENNY *(Off)*: I'm an accomplished sculptor, Marisol. Before that I was a Life and Growth Empowerment Practitioner. Before that I worked for the Brooklyn Spiritual Emergence Network.

(Lenny quickly reenters with his sculpture, a ball of nails welded together in a formless shape: it's an ugly little work of art and everyone knows it.)

This one's called "Marisol Perez." The nails symbolize all the things I know about you. Spaces between the nails are all the things I don't know about you. As you see, you're a great mystery . . .

(Marisol looks at the sculpture, trying hard to see some beauty in it.)

No one else is working like this. It's totally new. But it's only a small step in my career. I'm going to need a lot more *money* if I'm going to evolve past this point.

(Lenny looks hard at June. June buttons up her coat, hoping to avoid a confrontation.)

JUNE *(Tight)*: I don't think Marisol wants to hear us talk about money.

LENNY: Well, I'm not gonna get a job, June, so you can fuck that noise.

JUNE *(To Marisol)*: Who said "job"? When did I say "job"?

LENNY *(To Marisol)*: I promised myself to never work for anyone again. She heard me say that—

JUNE: Gee Lenny, fuck you, we're going—

(June starts to go. Lenny blocks her path to the door.)

LENNY *(To June)*: Why do you hate my sculpture? Why do you hate everything I do?!

JUNE *(Trying to control herself)*: Man, man . . . Lenny . . . you don't want to learn *anything* from me, do you? You want to be a pathetic invertebrate your whole life long. Fine. Just don't waste my precious time!

LENNY: Who gives a fuck about your time, I HAVE PROJECTS!

JUNE: Yeah? What ever happened to the CIA, Lenny? Didn't they want you for something *really special* in Nicaragua? What about the electric guitars you were gonna design for the Stones? What about *Smegma, the Literary Magazine of Brooklyn*? Huh?

(Lenny runs back into his offstage room.)

I swear, the cadavers of your dead projects are all over this goddamn apartment like Greenwood Cemetery. I can't eat a bowl of cereal in the morning without the ghosts of your old ideas begging me for a glass of milk!

(Lenny reenters with stacks of homemade magazines and several unusual homemade guitars. He throws this trash at June's feet.)

LENNY: *You wish Mom had drowned me!* I know that's what you wish! Well, you don't have to feel sorry for me anymore!

JUNE: Sure I do. You're pathetic. The only thing separating you from a concrete bed on Avenue D is *me*.

LENNY *(To Marisol)*: She thinks I'm a loser, Marisol! Can you believe that? Sometimes I want to kill her!

JUNE: Oh get out of my face, Lenny. You're never gonna kill me. You're never gonna get it together to kill *anybody*—

(Lenny exits into his offstage room again. June turns to Marisol angrily.)

Can I list for you just a few of the things I don't have because I have him? Lasting friendships. A retirement account. A house. A career. A nightlife. Winter clothing. Interest on checking. Regular real sex.

(Lenny returns with a long kitchen knife and tries to cut June's throat. June and Marisol scream.)

LENNY: *I was supposed to be somebody!* That's what I learned right after I died!

JUNE: YOU NEVER DIED!

(June scrambles from Lenny and goes for the door. There's chaos as Marisol starts throwing things at Lenny and Lenny continues to chase June. Lenny pulls June from the door and throws her back in the room.)

LENNY: The doctors all said I died! There's medical evidence! It's on the charts! My heart stopped for seven minutes and my soul was outta Lenox Hill at the speed of light!

(Lenny is almost out of control as he stalks June, slashing the air.)

JUNE: Your whole *life*, everything I do is to *bolster* you, build you up—

LENNY: After my death . . . my soul was cruising up and up . . . and it was intercepted by angels and sucked back into my body, *and I lived*!

MARISOL: Give me that knife!

LENNY: . . . I was resurrected, I returned to the living to warn the world that big changes are coming . . . and we have to be ready . . . *(Fighting tears)* I've been warning people for years, but no one listens to me . . .

(Lenny starts to cry. Marisol and June jump him, grabbing the knife away. Lenny throws himself on the ground like a toddler in a rage and cries. June and Marisol look at him.

It takes June a moment to catch her breath and gather her thoughts.)

JUNE: I can't do this shit no more. I can't mother you. Carry you around protected in my Epic Uterus anymore. This is final. Biology says you're a grown man. I don't love the law of the jungle, Lenny, but you're adult, you're leaving the nest and living in the real world from now on, eat or be eaten, I'm sorry, that's the way my emotions are built right now 'cause you *architectured* it that way! *(Beat)* I'm calling our mother, tell her not to take you in either. This is not a transition, Leonard. This is a break. A severing. So get up. Collect your mutant trash. Give me your fucking keys. Leave right now. And don't look back at me or I'll turn you to salt right where you stand with my eyes, so help me God.

(Lenny stands, gathers his trash and exits to his room. Marisol goes to comfort June but she's interrupted by Lenny reentering, wearing a coat, carrying a bag of golf clubs.

June gives Lenny all the money she has on her. Marisol is unable to look at Lenny. He turns angrily to June.)

LENNY: I almost had Marisol married to me, June. We practically had babies! Now I'm alone. Whatever happens to me out there, it's totally, specifically, on you.

(Lenny leaves the apartment. June sits at the table. Marisol looks at June.)

MARISOL: So where do you want to have dinner?

(No answer. Marisol sits with June, takes her hand. Tears on June's face.)

JUNE: You think I'm a shit for throwing him out . . . ?

MARISOL: Maybe people will throw him some change. Maybe this will force him to get a job.

JUNE: . . . is he gonna dissolve in the fucking street air . . . ?

(June runs to the door. She calls out.)

Lenny! I'm SORRY! Come back, I'm sorry!!

(No answer. June sits.)

Shit.

(June looks at Marisol, wiping her tears, getting an idea:)

You wanna live with me? 'Cause if you wanna live with me, in Lenny's empty bedroom, I'll rent it to you, it's available right away.

(Marisol smiles, surprised.)

MARISOL: Wait—where did that come from?

JUNE: Hey c'mon girlfriend, they're killing Marisol Perezes left and right today, we gotta stick together!

MARISOL *(Wanting to)*: Wow. I don't know what to say . . .

JUNE: You think the Bronx needs you? It doesn't. It needs blood. It needs to feed. You *wanna* be the blood supply for its filthy habits?

MARISOL: But the Bronx is where I'm from.

JUNE: So friggin' what? Come here. We'll survive the millennium as a team. I'll shop. You can clean the chemicals off the food. I know where to buy gas masks. You know the vocabulary on the street. We'll walk each other through land mines and sharpen each other's wits.

(Marisol smiles and looks at June.)

MARISOL: You're not saying that just because you're scared to be alone, right? You really want me here, right?

JUNE: Of course I do, hey.

MARISOL: Then let's do it, girlfriend.

(Delighted, June embraces Marisol.)

JUNE: Oh great!

(June and Marisol hold each other. June is about ready to cry. Marisol gently rocks her a little bit, then looks at June.)

MARISOL: I'm gonna go home and pack right now. We have to be fast. This town knows when you're alone. That's when it sends out the ghouls and the death squads.

(June nods understandingly, kisses Marisol and gives her Lenny's keys.)

JUNE: What a day I'm having, huh?

(Marisol takes the keys, leaves, goes back to her own apartment and immediately starts packing.)

Scene Seven

Later that night. Marisol is in the Bronx, packing. Her singing is heard underneath the others' dialogue.

MARISOL *(Softly)*:
   Madre que linda noche
   cuantas estrellas
   abreme la ventana
   que quiero verlas . . .

(June sits at the table in her apartment, facing downstage. She talks to herself.)

JUNE: Maybe someone'll throw Lenny some change, right?

(Lenny appears upstage, on the street, warming his hands at a burning trash can. His clothes are filthy and his eyes are glazed. The golf club is at his side. He looks at Marisol.)

LENNY: I've been on the street, Marisol. I know what it's like.

JUNE: Yeah, maybe people will throw him some change.

MARISOL *(Smiling, remembering)*: "The flat vowels . . ."

LENNY: It's incredible there. Logic was executed by firing squad. People tell passionate horror stories and other people stuff their faces and go on. The street breeds new species. And new silence. No spoken language works there. There are no verbs to describe the cold air as it sucks on your hands. And if there *were* words to describe it, Marisol, you wouldn't believe it anyway, because, in fact, it's literally unbelievable, it's another reality, and it's actually happening *right now*. And *that* fact— the fact that it's happening right *now*—compounds the unbelievable nature of the street, Marisol, adds to its lunacy, its permanent deniability. *(Beat)* But I know it's real. I've been bitten by it. I have its rabies.

JUNE: I know someone will throw him some change.

(Lenny raises the golf club over June's head. June is frozen. Blackout everywhere but Marisol's apartment. June and Lenny exit in the dark.)

Scene Eight

There's loud knocking at Marisol's door. Marisol stops packing and looks at the door. The knocking continues—loud, violent—louder.

MARISOL: Who is it?

(Before Marisol can move, her door is kicked open. Lenny comes in wielding a bloody golf club and holding an armful of exotic wildflowers.)

LENNY: So how can you live in this neighborhood? Huh? You got a death wish, you stupid woman?

MARISOL: What are you doing here?

(Marisol goes to her bed and scrambles for the knife underneath her pillow.)

LENNY: Don't you love yourself? Is that why you stay in this ghetto? Jesus, I almost got killed getting here!

(Marisol points the knife at Lenny.)

MARISOL: Get out or I'll rip out both your fucking eyes, Lenny!

LENNY: God, I missed you.

(Lenny closes the door and locks all the locks.)

MARISOL: This is not going to happen to me in my own house! I still have God's protection!

(Lenny holds out the flowers.)

LENNY: Here. I hadda break into the Bronx Botanical Garden for them, but they match your eyes . . .

(Lenny hands Marisol the flowers.)

MARISOL: Okay—thank you—okay—why don't we—turn around—and go—down to Brooklyn—okay?—let's go talk to June—

LENNY: We can't. Impossible. June *isn't*. Is *not*. I don't know who she is anymore! She's out walking the streets of Brooklyn! Babbling like an idiot! Looking for her lost mind!

MARISOL: What do you mean? Where is she?

LENNY: She had an accident. Her head had an accident. With the golf club. It was weird.

MARISOL *(Looking at the bloody club)*: What did you do to her?

LENNY: She disappeared! I don't know!

MARISOL *(Panicking)*: Please tell me June's okay, Lenny. Tell me she's not in some body bag somewhere—

LENNY: Oh man, you saw what it's like! June *controlled* me. She had me *neutered*. I squatted and stooped and served like a goddamn house eunuch!

MARISOL: Did you hurt her?

(Lenny starts to cry. He sobs like a baby, his body wracked with grief and self-pity.)

LENNY: There are whole histories of me you can't guess. Did you know I was a medical experiment? To fix my asthma when I was five, my mother volunteered me for a free experimental drug on an army base in Nevada. *I was a shrieking experiment in army medicine for six years!* Isn't that funny? *(He laughs, trying to fight his tears)* And that drug's made me so friggin' loopy, I can't hold down a job, make friends, get a degree, *nothing*—and June?—June's had *everything*. She loved you. That's why she never brought you home to meet me *even after I begged her for two years.*

(Marisol is silent—and that silence nearly makes him explode.)

DON'T BE THIS WAY. We don't have to be enemies. We can talk to each other the right way—

MARISOL: We have no right way, Lenny.

(Lenny jumps up and down, very happy.)

LENNY: We do! We do! 'Cause we have *God*, Marisol. We have God in common. Maybe it's God's will I'm with you now. On this frontier. Out in this lawless city, I'm what he designed for you.

MARISOL: I don't know what you're talking about . . .

LENNY: It's why God brought me here tonight—to offer you a way to survive. I know you don't love me. But you can't turn your back on God's gift.

MARISOL *(Exhausted)*: Jesus Christ, just tell me what you want . . .

(Lenny moves closer.)

LENNY: I want to offer you a deal. *(Beat)* You controlled your life
until now. But your life's in shambles! Ruins! So I'm gonna
let you give *me* control over your life. That means I'll do
everything for you. I'll take responsibility. I'll get a job and
make money. I'll name our children. Okay? And what you
get in return is my protection.

(Beat. Lenny gives Marisol the golf club.)

I can protect you like June did. I can keep out the criminals
and carry the knife for you. I can be your guardian angel,
Marisol.

MARISOL: You're asking—

LENNY: A small price. Your faith. Your pretty Puerto Rican smile.
No. I don't even want to sleep with you anymore. I don't
want your affection. Or your *considerable* sexual mystery. I
just want you to look up to me. Make me big. Make me central. Praise me, feed me, and believe everything I tell you.

(Lenny steps closer to Marisol.)

You once tried to give these things to June. And June would
have said yes because she loved you. Well, I'm June. June and
I are here, together, under this hungry skin. You can love us
both, Marisol.

*(Marisol looks at Lenny a long moment, studying him, thinking
of a way out. She makes a decision. She tosses her knife on the
bed and drops the golf club.
    She takes a step toward Lenny. They stare at each other.
Marisol lets herself be embraced. Lenny, amazed, revels in the
feel of her body against his.)*

MARISOL: Okay. I'll believe what you say. I'll live inside you.

(Lenny is oblivious to everything but Marisol's warm hands. She kisses him. It's the most electrifying feeling Lenny's ever known. He closes his eyes.)

But. Before we set up house—live happily ever after—we're going to go outside—you and me—and we're going to find out what happened to your sister . . .

LENNY *(Oblivious)*: She's lost. She can't be found.

MARISOL *(Kissing him)*: . . . that's my condition . . .

(Lenny starts to push Marisol to the bed. She starts to resist.)

LENNY: It's too dangerous for a girl out there.

MARISOL: . . . but if you don't help me find her, Lenny . . . there's no deal . . .

(He pushes her. She resists. Lenny looks at her, hurt, a little confused.)

LENNY: But I don't want to share you.

(Beat.)

MARISOL: Too bad. That's the deal.

(Beat.)

LENNY *(Hurt, realizing)*: You don't love me. You're just fucking with me. That's not okay! WELL, I'M GLAD I HIT HER!

(Lenny grabs Marisol. Marisol tries to escape. He holds her tightly, trying to kiss her. He throws her to the floor. He rips at her clothes, trying to tear them off. Marisol struggles with all her strength—until she finally pulls free and goes for the golf club. He tries to grab it from her and she swings at him.)

You're lying to me! Why are you always lying to me?!

MARISOL: Because you're the enemy, Lenny. I will always be your enemy, because you will always find a way to be out there, hiding in stairwells, behind doors, under the blankets in my bed, in the cracks of every bad dream I've had since I've known there were savage differences between girls and boys! And I know you'll always be hunting for me. And I'll never be able to relax, or stop to look at the sky, or smile at something beautiful on the street—

LENNY: But I'm just a guy trying to be happy too—

MARISOL: I want you to tell me, RIGHT NOW, where June is— *right now*!

(Marisol swings at Lenny. He panics and falls to his knees in front of her. Marisol pounds the floor with the golf club.)

LENNY: She's on the street.

MARISOL: Where?

LENNY: Brooklyn.

MARISOL: Where?

LENNY: I don't know!

MARISOL: What happened?

LENNY: I hit her on the head. She doesn't know who she is. She went out there to look for you.

(Marisol stands over him, poised to strike him. He's shaking with fear.)

Look at me. I'm a mess on the floor. Just asking you to look at me. To give me compassion and let me live like a human being for once. Marisol, we could have a baby . . . and love it so much . . .

(Marisol only shakes her head in disgust and turns to the door. Lenny springs to his feet and lunges at her. She turns and swings the club and hits Lenny.
He falls to the ground.
Marisol looks at Lenny's fallen body. Has she killed him? She panics and runs out of the apartment with the golf club.
Blackout everywhere except on the street area.)

Scene Nine

Marisol runs to the street area.

It starts to snow there. There's blood on Marisol's clothes. She's extremely cold. She shivers. She kneels on the ground, alone, not knowing what to do or where to go.

Lights up over Marisol's head, against the brick wall. The Angel appears. The Angel wears regulation military fatigues, complete with face camouflage and medals. She looks like a soldier about to go into battle. The Uzi is strapped to her back.

Marisol sees her and gasps.

There's blood coming down the Angel's back: the Angel has taken off her silver wings—her wings of peace. She holds the bloody wings out to the audience, like an offering. Then she drops the wings. They float down to the street.

Marisol picks them up.

MARISOL: War?

(The wings dissolve in Marisol's hands. Blackout everywhere.)

ACT TWO

Darkness. All the interiors are gone. The entire set now consists of the brick wall and a huge surreal street that covers the entire stage.

The Angel is gone. The gold crown is still there.

Street lighting comes up but there's something very different about this light. On this street, reality has been altered—and this new reality is reflected in the lighting.

We see a metal trash bin, overflowing with trash, and a fire hydrant covered in rosaries. There are several large mounds of rags on stage; underneath each mound is a sleeping homeless person.

Marisol is onstage exactly where she was at the end of Act One. She's holding out her hands as if holding the Angel's wings but they're gone now; she holds air.

She looks around and notices that the street she's now on is nothing like the street she remembers. She registers this weird difference and picks up the golf club, ready to defend herself.

She looks up to see the Angel, but she's gone.

She thinks she hears a sound behind her. She swings the club. There's nothing there. She tries to orient herself but she can't tell north from south.

And even though it's the dead of winter, it's also much warmer than it was before. Startled, Marisol fans herself.

Bright sparkling lights streak across the sky like tracers or comets. The lights are followed by distant rumblings. Is that a thunderclap?

Or an explosion? Marisol hits the ground. Then the lights stop. Silence.

The Woman With Furs enters. The Woman is prosperous: long fur coat and high heels—but there are subtle bruises and cuts on her face and it looks like there's dried blood on her coat. She stands to the side, very, very still. She holds an open newspaper, but she stares past it, no emotion on her shell-shocked face.

Marisol looks at the Woman With Furs, hesitates, then goes to her.

MARISOL: Excuse me. Miss?

(No answer from the Woman With Furs, who doesn't look at her.)

Where the hell are we?

(The Woman With Furs ignores her. Marisol gets closer.)

I'm—supposed to be on 180th Street. In the Bronx. There's supposed to be a bodega right *here*. A public school *there*. They sold crack on that corner. It was cold this morning!

(The Woman With Furs speaks out to the air, as if in a trance.)

WOMAN WITH FURS: God help you, you get in my face.

(Marisol begins to examine the altered space with growing fear.)

MARISOL: No buildings. No streets. No cars. No noise. No cops. There are no subway tokens in my pocket!

WOMAN WITH FURS: I have no money.

MARISOL *(Realizing)*: It's what she said would happen, isn't it? She said she'd drop her wings of peace . . . and I wouldn't recognize the world . . .

WOMAN WITH FURS: Don't you know where you are either?

MARISOL *(Trying to think it through)*: . . . I have to . . . I have to . . . reclaim what I know: I need June. Where's June? Brooklyn. South. I gotta go south, find my friend, and restore her broken mind.

(Marisol tries to run away, hoping to find the subway to Brooklyn, but it's impossible to find anything familiar in this radically altered landscape.)

WOMAN WITH FURS: I had tickets to *Les Misérables*. But I took a wrong turn. Followed bad advice. Ended up on this weird street.

(Marisol sees something in the distance that makes her freeze in her tracks.)

MARISOL *(To herself)*: The Empire State Building? . . . *what's it doing over there?* It's supposed to be south. But that's . . . north . . . I'm sure it is . . . isn't it?

(In her panic, Marisol runs to the Woman With Furs and tries to grab her arm.)

You have to help me!

(The Woman With Furs instantly recoils from Marisol's touch. She starts to wander away.)

WOMAN WITH FURS: I have to go. But I can't find a cab. I can't seem to find any transportation.
MARISOL: You're not listening! There's no transportation; forget that; the city's *gone.* You have to help me. We have to go south together and protect each other.

(Marisol grabs the Woman With Furs's arm roughly, trying to pull her offstage. The Woman With Furs seems to snap out of her trance and pull back. The Woman With Furs is suddenly shaking, tearful, like a caged animal.)

WOMAN WITH FURS: Oh God, I thought you were a nice person!
MARISOL *(Grabbing the Woman)*: I *am* a nice person, but I've had some bad luck—
WOMAN WITH FURS *(Struggling)*: Oh God, you're hurting me—

MARISOL *(Letting go)*: No, no, no, I'm okay; I don't belong out here; I have a job in publishing; I'm middle-class—

WOMAN WITH FURS *(Freaking out, pointing at golf club)*: Oh please don't kill me like that barbarian killed Marisol Perez!

(Marisol lets the Woman With Furs go. The Woman With Furs is almost crying.)

MARISOL: I'm not what you think.

WOMAN WITH FURS: . . . Oh God, why did I have to buy that fucking hat?! God . . . God . . . why?

MARISOL: Please. June's not used to the street, she's an indoor animal, like a cat . . .

WOMAN WITH FURS: I bought a fucking hat on credit and everything disintegrated!

MARISOL: South. Protection.

(The Woman With Furs takes off her fur coat. Underneath, she wears ripped pajamas. We can see the bruises and cuts on her arms clearly.)

WOMAN WITH FURS: There is no protection. I just got out of hell. Last month, I was two hundred dollars over my credit card limit because I bought a hat on sale. And you know they're cracking down on that kind of thing. I used to do it all the time. It didn't matter. But now it matters. Midnight. The police came. Grabbed me out of bed, waving my credit statement in my face, my children screaming, they punched my husband in the stomach. I told them I was a lawyer! With a house in Cos Cob! And personal references a mile long! But they hauled me to this . . . huge windowless brick building in Brooklyn . . . where they tortured me . . . they . . .

(The Woman With Furs cries. Marisol goes to her and covers her up with the fur coat. Marisol holds her.)

MARISOL: That can't happen.

WOMAN WITH FURS: A lot of things can't happen that are happening. Everyone I know's had terrible luck this year. Losing condos. Careers cut in half. Ending up on the street. I thought I'd be immune. I thought I'd be safe.

MARISOL: This is going to sound crazy. But I think I know why this is happening.

(The Woman With Furs looks at Marisol, suddenly very afraid.)

WOMAN WITH FURS: No. No.

(The Woman With Furs tries to get away from Marisol. Marisol stops her.)

MARISOL: It's angels, isn't it? It's the war.

WOMAN WITH FURS *(Panicking)*: God is great! God is good! It didn't happen! It didn't happen! I dreamed it! I lied!

MARISOL: It did! It happened to me!

WOMAN WITH FURS: I'm not going to talk about this! You're going to think I'm crazy too! You're going to tell the Citibank MasterCard people where I am so they can pick me up and torture me some more!

MARISOL: I wouldn't!

(The Woman With Furs grabs the golf club out of Marisol's hand.)

WOMAN WITH FURS: I know what I'm going to do now. I'm going to turn *you* in. I'm going to tell the Citibank police you stole my plastic! They'll like me for that. They'll like me a lot. They'll restore my banking privileges!

(The Woman With Furs starts swinging wildly at Marisol. Marisol dodges the Woman With Furs.)

MARISOL: I am not an animal! I am not a barbarian! I don't fight at this level!

WOMAN WITH FURS *(Swinging)*: Welcome to the new world order, babe!

(The Man With Scar Tissue enters in a wheelchair. He's a home-less man in shredded, burnt rags. He wears a hood that covers his head and obscures his face. He wears sunglasses and gloves. His wheelchair is full of plastic garbage bags, clothes, books, news-papers, bottles, junk.)

SCAR TISSUE: It's getting so bad, a guy can't sleep under the stars anymore.

(The Woman With Furs sees the Man With Scar Tissue and stops swinging.)

WOMAN WITH FURS *(Indicating Marisol)*: This brown piece of shit is mine! *I'm* going to turn her in! Not you!

SCAR TISSUE: I was sleeping under the constellations one night and my whole life changed, took *seconds*: I had a life—then bingo—I *didn't* have a life . . . *(He moves toward the Woman With Furs)* . . . maybe you got it, huh? You got the thing I need . . .

WOMAN WITH FURS: Homelessness is against the law in this city. I'm going to have you two arrested! They'll like that. I'll get big points for that! I'll be revitalized!

(The Woman With Furs runs off with the golf club.
Man With Scar Tissue looks at Marisol. He waves hello. She looks at him—wary, but grateful—and tries to smile. She's instantly aware of his horrendous smell.)

MARISOL: She, she was trying to kill me . . . thank you . . .

SCAR TISSUE: Used to be able to sleep under the moon *unmolested.* Moon was a shield. Catching all the bad karma before it fell to earth. All those crater holes in the moon? Those ain't rocks! That's bad karma crashing to the moon's surface!

MARISOL *(Really shaken)*: She thinks I belong out here, but I don't. I'm well educated . . . anyone can see that . . .

SCAR TISSUE: Now the moon's gone. The shield's been lifted. Shit falls on you randomly. Sleep outside, you're fucked. That's why I got this! Gonna *yank* the moon back!

(From inside his wheelchair, Scar Tissue pulls out a magnet. He aims his magnet to the sky and waits for the moon to appear.)

MARISOL: She's crazy, that's all! I have to go before she comes back.

(Marisol starts going back and forth, looking for south.)

SCAR TISSUE: Good thing I'm not planning to get married. What would a honeymoon be like now? Some stupid cardboard cut-out dangling out your hotel window? What kind of inspiration is that? How's a guy supposed to get it up for *that*?

(Scar Tissue fondles himself, hoping to manufacture a hard-on, but nothing happens and he gives up.)

MARISOL *(Noticing what he's doing)*: I have to get to Brooklyn. I'm looking for my friend. She has red hair.
SCAR TISSUE: And did you know the moon carries the souls of dead people up to Heaven? Uh-huh. The new moon is dark and empty and gets filled with new glowing souls—until it's a bright full moon—then it carries its silent burden to God . . .
MARISOL: Do you know which way is south?!

(Marisol continues to walk around and around the stage, looking hopelessly for any landmark that will tell her which way is south. Scar Tissue watches her, holding his magnet up.)

SCAR TISSUE: Give it up, princess. Time is crippled. Geography's deformed. You're permanently lost out here!
MARISOL: Bullshit. Even if God is senile, He still cares, He doesn't play dice you know. I read that.
SCAR TISSUE: Shit, what century do *you* live in?

(Marisol keeps running around the stage.)

MARISOL: June and I had plans. Gonna live together. Survive together. I gotta get her fixed! I gotta get Lenny buried!

(Scar Tissue laughs and suddenly drops his magnet and jumps out of his wheelchair. He runs to Marisol, stopping her in her tracks. He looks at the shocked Marisol fully for the first time. He smiles, very pleased.)

SCAR TISSUE: You look pretty nice. You're kinda cute, in fact. What do you think this all means, us two, a man and woman, bumping into each other like this?

MARISOL *(Wary)*: I don't know. But thank you for helping me. Maybe my luck hasn't run out.

SCAR TISSUE *(Laughs)*: Oh, don't trust luck! Fastest way to die around here. Trust gunpowder. Trust plutonium. Don't trust divine intervention or you're fucked. My name is Elvis Presley, beautiful, what's yours?

MARISOL *(Wary)*: . . . Marisol Perez.

(Scar Tissue nearly jumps out of his rags.)

SCAR TISSUE: *What?!!* No! Your name can't be that! Can't be Marisol Perez!

MARISOL: It is. It has to be.

SCAR TISSUE: You're confused! Or are the goddamn graves coughing up the dead?!

MARISOL: I'm not dead! That was her! I'm—me!

SCAR TISSUE: You can't prove it!

MARISOL: I was born in the Bronx. But—but—I can't remember the street!

SCAR TISSUE: A-ha! Dead!

MARISOL *(A recitation, an effort)*: Born 1966—lived on East Tremont—then Taylor Avenue—Grand Concourse—Mami died—Fordham—English major—Phi Beta Kappa—I went into science publishing—I'm a head copywriter—I make good money—I work with words—I'm clean . . . *(She holds her head and closes her eyes)* I lived in the Bronx . . . I commuted light-years to this other planet called—Manhattan! I learned new vocabularies . . . wore weird native dress . . . mastered arcane rituals . . . and amputated neat sections of my psyche, my cultural heritage . . . yeah, clean easy amputations

... with no pain expressed at all—none!—but so much pain kept inside I almost choked on it ... so far deep inside my Manhattan bosses and Manhattan friends and my broken Bronx consciousness never even suspected ...

(As Marisol recites facts, Scar Tissue starts going through his bag, pulling out old magazines and newspapers. He reads from the New York Post:)

SCAR TISSUE: "Memorial services for Marisol Perez were held this morning in Saint Patrick's Cathedral. The estimated fifty thousand mourners included the Mayor of New York, the Bronx Borough President, the Guardian Angels, and the cast of the popular daytime soap opera *As the World Turns* ... "

MARISOL: She wasn't me! I'm me! And I'm outta here!

(Marisol starts to run off—but is stopped as, far upstage, in the dark, a Nazi skinhead walks by, holding a can of gasoline, goose-stepping ominously toward a sleeping homeless person. Marisol runs back and hides behind Scar Tissue's wheelchair. The Skinhead doesn't see them.
Scar Tissue sees the Skinhead and suddenly hides behind Marisol, shaking. He starts to whine and cry and moan. The homeless person runs off. The Skinhead exits, chasing the person. When the Skinhead is gone, Scar Tissue turns angrily to Marisol.)

SCAR TISSUE: Who are you for real and why do you attract so much trouble?! I hope you don't let those Nazis come near me!

MARISOL: I don't mean to—

(He grabs Marisol.)

SCAR TISSUE: What are you!? Are you protection? Are you benign? Or are you some kind of angel of death?

MARISOL: I'm a good person.

SCAR TISSUE: Then why don't you do something about those Nazis?! They're all over the place. I'm getting out of here—

(Scar Tissue tries to leave. Marisol stops him.)

MARISOL: Don't leave me!

SCAR TISSUE: Why? You're not alone, are you? You got your faith still intact. You still believe God is good. You still think you can glide through the world and not be part of it.

MARISOL: I'm not a Nazi!

SCAR TISSUE: I can't trust you. Ever since the angels went into open revolt, you can't trust your own mother . . . oops.

(Marisol looks at him.)

MARISOL: What did you say? You too? Did angels talk to you too?

SCAR TISSUE *(Worried)*: No. Never mind. I don't know a thing. Just talking out my ass.

MARISOL: You didn't dream it—

SCAR TISSUE *(Scared)*: I had enough punishment! I don't wanna get in the middle of some celestial Vietnam! I don't want any more angelic napalm dropped on me!

MARISOL: But I saw one too—I did—*what do all these visitations mean?*

(Marisol suddenly grabs Scar Tissue's hands—and he screams, pulls away, and cowers on the ground like a beaten dog.)

SCAR TISSUE: NOT MY HANDS! Don't touch my hands!

(Scar Tissue rips his gloves off. His hands are covered in burn scars. He blows on his boiling hands.)

MARISOL: Oh my God.

SCAR TISSUE *(Nearly crying)*: Heaven erupts but who pays the price? The fucking innocent do . . . !

MARISOL: What happened to you?

SCAR TISSUE *(Crying)*: I was an air-traffic controller, Marisol Perez. I had a life. Then I saw angels in the radar screen and I started to drink.

(Marisol gets closer to the whimpering Scar Tissue. She has yet to really see his face.

Marisol reaches out to him and pulls the hood back and removes his sunglasses. Scar Tissue's face has been horribly burned. She tries not to gasp but she can't help it.)

MARISOL: *Ay Dios, ay Dios mio, ay Dios . . .*

SCAR TISSUE: You're looking for your friend . . . everyone here is looking for something . . . I'm looking for something too . . .

MARISOL: What is it? Maybe I can help?

SCAR TISSUE: I'm looking for my lost skin. Have you seen my lost skin? It was once very pretty. We were very close. I was really attached to it.

(Scar Tissue runs to the trash bin and starts looking through it.)

MARISOL: I haven't seen anything like that.

SCAR TISSUE: It's got to be somewhere . . . it must be looking for me . . . it must be lonely too, don't you think . . . ?

MARISOL: Look, I'm sorry I bothered you, I'm, I'm going to go now . . .

(Scar Tissue looks at Marisol.)

SCAR TISSUE: I was just sleeping under the stars. It was another night when I couldn't find shelter. The places I went to, I got beat up. They took my clothes. Urinated in my mouth. Fucking blankets they gave me were laced with DDT. I said Fuck It, I took my shit outside and went up to some dick-head park in the Bronx . . .

MARISOL *(Remembering)*: Van Cortlandt Park?

SCAR TISSUE: . . . just to be near some shriveled trees and alone and away from the massive noise, just for a little nap . . . my eyes closed . . . I vaguely remember the sound of goose-stepping teenagers from Staten Island with a can of gasoline, shouting orders in German . . .

(Marisol walks away from Scar Tissue.)

MARISOL: June's waiting for me . . .

SCAR TISSUE: A flash of light. I exploded outward. My bubbling skin divorced my suffering nerves and ran away, looking for some coolness, some paradise, some other body to embrace! *(Laughs bitterly)* Now I smell like barbecue! I could have eaten myself! I could have charged money for pieces of my broiled meat!

MARISOL: Please stop. I get the picture.

(Scar Tissue stops, looks at Marisol sadly. He motions to her that he needs help. She helps him with his gloves, sunglasses, hood.)

SCAR TISSUE: The angel was Japanese. Dressed in armor. Dressed in iron. Dressed to endure the fire of war. She had a scimitar.

MARISOL *(Can't believe it; wanting to)*: She?

SCAR TISSUE: Kissed me. I almost exploded. I kept hearing Jimi Hendrix in my middle ear as those lips, like two *brands*, nearly melted me. She was radiant. Raw.

MARISOL AND SCAR TISSUE: Fulgent.

SCAR TISSUE: She told me when angels are bored at night, they write your nightmares. She said the highest among the angels carry God's throne on their backs for eternity, singing, "Glory, glory, glory!" But her message was terrible and after she kissed me . . .

MARISOL AND SCAR TISSUE: . . . I spit at her.

SCAR TISSUE: Was that the right thing to do, Marisol?

MARISOL: I thought it was . . . but I don't know.

(Marisol looks gently at Scar Tissue. She kisses him softly. He smiles and pats her on the head like a puppy. He goes to his wheelchair and pulls out an old bottle of Kentucky bourbon. He smiles and offers the bottle to Marisol.

Marisol drinks greedily. Scar Tissue applauds her. She smiles as the hot liquid burns down her throat. She laughs long and loud: in this barren landscape, it's a beautiful sound.

As they both laugh, Scar Tissue motions that they should embrace. Marisol holds her breath and embraces him.)

SCAR TISSUE *(Hopeful)*: So? Feelin' horny? Can I hope?

(Marisol quickly lets him go, and gives him back his bottle.)

MARISOL: Let's not push it, okay Elvis?

(Scar Tissue laughs. He goes to his wheelchair and prepares to hit the road again.)

SCAR TISSUE: Word on the street is, water no longer seeks its own level, there are fourteen inches to the foot, six days in the week, seven planets in the solar system, and the French are polite. I also hear the sun rises in the north and sets in the south. I think I saw the sun setting over there . . . instinct tells me south is over there . . .

(Marisol turns to face south.)

MARISOL: Thank you.

(The Skinhead crosses the stage again, with the can of gasoline, chasing the frightened homeless person. Marisol and Scar Tissue hit the ground.
  The homeless person falls. The Skinhead pours the gasoline on the homeless person and lights a match. There's a scream as the homeless person burns to death. Marisol covers her ears so she can't hear.
  The Skinhead exits. Marisol and Scar Tissue quickly get up. Marisol tries to run to the burnt homeless person. Scar Tissue stops her.)

SCAR TISSUE: No! There's nothing you can do! Don't even look!
MARISOL: Oh my God . . .
SCAR TISSUE: I gotta get outta here. Look—if you see some extra skin laying around somewhere . . . pick it up for me, okay? I'll be exceedingly grateful. Bye.

(Scar Tissue gets back into his wheelchair.)

MARISOL: Why don't we stay together—protect each other?

SCAR TISSUE: There is no protection. That Nazi is after me. He works for TRW. If I stay . . . you're gonna have torturers and death squads all over you.

(Marisol goes toward him.)

MARISOL: I'm not afraid—

SCAR TISSUE: No, I said! *Get away from me! Just get away from me!! Are you fucking CRAZY OR WHAT?* Just—just if you see my skin, beautiful . . . have some good sex with it and tell it to come home quick. *(He's gone. From offstage:)* I'll always love you, Marisol!

(Marisol is alone. More odd streaking lights rake the sky. Marisol hits the ground again, looking up, hoping that the barrage will end.)

MARISOL *(To herself)*: South—that way—I'll go south that way, where the sun sets, to look for June until I hit Miami— then—I'll know I passed her.

(The streaking lights stop. Marisol gets up. She takes a step. Then another step. With each step, the lights change as if she were entering a new part of the city or time has suddenly jumped forward.

She finds some homeless person's old coat and puts it on.)

I'm getting dirty . . . and my clothes smell bad . . . I'm getting dirty and my clothes smell bad . . . my fucking stomach's grumbling . . .

(Marisol runs up to the metal trash bin. She ducks behind it. She takes a piss. She finishes and comes out from behind the trash bin, relieved. Grabbing her empty stomach, Marisol tries to think through her predicament. To the gold crown:)

Okay, I just wanna go home. I just wanna live with June—want my boring nine-to-five back—my two-weeks-out-of-the-year vacation—my intellectual detachment—my ability to read about the misery of the world and not lose a moment out of my busy day. To believe you really knew what you were doing, God—please—if the sun would just come *up*! *(Beat. To herself:)* But what if the sun doesn't come up? And this is it? It's the deadline. I'm against the wall. I'm at the rim of the apocalypse . . .

(Marisol looks up. To the angel:)

Blessed guardian angel! Maybe you were right. God has stopped looking. We can't live life as if nothing's changed. To live in the sweet past. To look backwards for our instructions. We have to reach up, beyond the debris, past the future, spit in the eye of the sun, make a fist, and say *no*, and say *no*, and say *no*, and say . . . *(Beat. Doubts. To herself:)* . . . no, what if she's wrong?

(She hurriedly gets on her knees to pray. Vicious, to the crown:)

Dear God, All-Powerful, All-Beautiful, what do I do now? How do I get out of this? Do I have to make a deal? Arrange payment and bail myself out? *What about it!?* I'll do anything! I'll spy for you. I'll steal for you. I'll decipher strange angelic codes and mine harbors and develop germ bombs and poison the angelic food supply. DEAR GOD, WHO DO I HAVE TO BETRAY TO GET OUT OF THIS FUCKING MESS?!

(It starts to snow lightly. Marisol can't believe it. She holds out her hand.)

Snow? It's eighty degrees!

(We hear the sound of bombs, heavy artillery, very close. Marisol is suddenly, violently, gripped by hunger pains. She grabs her stomach.)

Oh God!

(Marisol scrambles to the trash bin and starts burrowing into it like an animal searching for food. She finally finds a paper bag. She tears it open. She finds a bunch of moldy French fries. She closes her eyes and prepares to eat them.)

LENNY'S VOICE: Marisol you don't want to eat that!

(Marisol throws the food down.)

MARISOL *(To herself)*: Lenny?

(Lenny comes in pushing a battered baby carriage full of junk. Lenny is nine months pregnant: huge belly, swollen breasts. Marisol is stunned by the transformation.)

Holy shit.
LENNY: Don't eat anything in that pile, Marisol. It's lethal.
MARISOL: You're alive and you're . . . bloated—
LENNY: Man who owned the restaurant on the other side of that wall put rat poison in the trash to discourage the homeless from picking through the pile. God bless the child that's got his own, huh? It's nice to see you again, Marisol.

(It stops snowing. Staring at his stomach, Marisol goes over to Lenny.)

MARISOL *(Amazed)*: I thought I killed you.
LENNY: Almost. But I forgive you. I forgive my sister, too.
MARISOL: You've seen her?
LENNY: I haven't seen her, sorry. Hey, you want food? I have a little food. I'll prepare you some secret edible food.

(Marisol goes to Lenny, wide-eyed.)

MARISOL: Okay . . . but . . . Lenny . . . you're immense . . .

(Marisol helps Lenny sit. He motions for her to sit next to him.)

LENNY: I'm fucking enormous. Got the worst hemorrhoids. The smell of Chinese food makes me puke my guts.

MARISOL *(Embarrassed)*: I just don't know . . . what to think about this . . . and what would June say . . . ?

LENNY *(Chuckles)*: I have something you're gonna like, Marisol. Took me great pains to get. Lots of weaseling around the black market, greasing palms, you know, giving blow jobs—*the things a parent will do for their fetus!*—until I got it . . .

(Lenny produces a bag. In the bag, Lenny reveals a scrawny little apple wrapped lovingly in layer after layer of delicate colored paper. Marisol can't believe what she sees.)

MARISOL: That's an apple. But that's extinct.

LENNY: Only if you believe the networks. Powers that be got the very last tree. It's in the Pentagon. In the center of the five-sided beast.

(Lenny bites the apple, relishing its flavor. He pats his stomach approvingly. Marisol hungrily watches him eat.)

I was on a terrible diet 'til I got knocked up. Eating cigarette butts, old milk cartons, cat food, raw shoelaces, roach motels. It's nice to be able to give my baby a few essential vitamins.

MARISOL: You're really gonna be a mother?

LENNY: Baby's been kicking. It's got great aim. Always going for my bladder. I'm pissing every five minutes.

MARISOL *(Tentative)*: Can I feel?

(Marisol puts her hand on Lenny's belly. She feels movement and pulls her hand away.)

LENNY: It's impossible to sleep. Lying on my back, I'm crushed. On my side, I can't breathe. The baby's heartbeat keeps me up at night. The beating is dreadful. Sounds like a bomb. I know when it goes, it's gonna go BIG.

MARISOL *(Frightened, unsure)*: Something's moving in there . . .

LENNY: When it's in a good mood it does back flips and my fucking kidneys end up in my throat. Did I tell you about my hemorrhoids? Here, eat.

(Lenny gives Marisol the apple. She bites into it—chews—then quickly spits it all out. Livid, Lenny takes the apple away from Marisol.)

Don't waste my FOOD, *you dumb shit!*

(Lenny starts picking up the bits of half-chewed apple spit out by Marisol and eats them greedily. Marisol continues to spit.)

MARISOL *(Angry)*: It's just salt inside there . . . just *salt* . . .

LENNY: My baby's trying to build a brain! My baby needs all the minerals it can get!

MARISOL: It's not an apple! It's not food!

LENNY: Get outta here if you're gonna be ungrateful! My baby and I don't need you! *(He devours the apple and tries to keep from crying)* There isn't a single food group in the world that isn't pure salt anymore! Where the fuck have you been?! *(He holds his stomach for comfort)*

MARISOL: This is your old bullshit, Lenny. That's a fucking pumpkin you got under your clothes. A big bundle of deceit and sexual CONFUSION. You're trying to *dislodge* me. Finally push me over the *edge*. Contradict *all* I know so I won't be able to say my own *name*.

(Marisol angrily pushes Lenny and he topples over, holding his stomach.)

LENNY: There isn't much food left in the PENTAGON, you know!

MARISOL: Oh, give me a break. When the sun comes up in the morning, all this will be gone! The city will come back! People will go back to work. You'll be a myth. A folktale.

(Bitter) Maybe you should stop pretending you're pregnant and find a job.

LENNY: *How can you say that when this is your baby?!*

MARISOL: It's not my baby!

LENNY: For days and days all I did was think about you and think about you and the more I thought about you, the bigger I got! Of course it's yours!

MARISOL: I don't know what you're saying!

LENNY: I shouldda had a fucking *abortion* . . .

MARISOL *(Trying not to lose control)*: I think you're a freak, Lenny. I'm supposed to know that men don't have babies. But I don't know that anymore, do I? If you're really pregnant, then we have to start at the beginning, don't we? Well I'm not ready to do that!

(Lenny gets to his feet, indignant.)

LENNY: I'm no freak. Every man should have this experience. There'd be fewer wars. *This* is power. *This* is energy. I guard my expanding womb greedily. I worship my new organs . . . the violent bloodstream sending food and oxygen . . . back and forth . . . *between two hearts.* One body. Two surging hearts! *That's* a revolution!

(He starts off. He stops in his tracks. He drops everything. He grabs his stomach. Pain knocks out his breathing.)

MARISOL: Now what is it?

LENNY: Oh shit . . . I think it's time. I think this is it.

MARISOL: Get outta here.

(Lenny's pants are suddenly wet.)

LENNY: My water's burst. Oh God, it can't be now . . .

MARISOL: I'm telling you to stop this!

LENNY *(Panicking)*: I'm not ready. Feel my breasts! They're empty! I can't let this baby be born yet! What if my body can't make enough milk to feed my baby?!

(Lenny shrieks with pain, falls to his knees. Marisol helps him lie down. She kneels beside him.)

MARISOL: Okay, Lenny, breathe—breathe—breathe—
LENNY *(Incredible pain)*: I'm breathing, you ASSHOLE, I'm breathing!
MARISOL: Breathe more!
LENNY: Jesus and I thought *war* was hell!
MARISOL: Oh my God—oh Jesus . . .
LENNY: If I pull off this birth thing, *it'll be a miracle!*
MARISOL: . . . *Angel of God please help him!*

(Marisol quickly covers Lenny's abdomen with her coat. Lenny starts the final stage of labor. He bears down.
Lenny lets out a final, cataclysmic scream.
The baby is born. Marisol "catches" the baby.
Marisol holds the silent baby in the coat, wrapping it tight. She examines the baby. Lenny's huge stomach has disappeared. He breathes hard. Short silence.
Lenny sits up slowly, wiping sweat from his face, happy the ordeal is over. All Lenny wants to do is hold his child. Marisol stands up holding the baby, looking at it a long time, a troubled look on her face.
Lenny holds out his arms for the baby. Marisol looks at Lenny and shakes her head, sadly, no. Lenny looks at Marisol, all hope drained from his face.)

LENNY: Dead?
MARISOL: I'm sorry.

(Marisol nods yes and wraps the baby tighter.
Marisol gives Lenny his baby. Lenny takes the bundle, kisses it, holds back tears. Marisol looks at him.)

LENNY: C'mon. There's something we have to do now.

(Holding the baby, Lenny starts to walk around and around the stage. Marisol follows.

*They come to the downstage corner where the rosary-covered
fire hydrant is. Special lighting on this area. Marisol looks down
and notices little crucifixes scratched into the sidewalk in rows.
Dazzling, frenetic lights rip the air above Marisol and Lenny.)*

Do you know where you are, Marisol?

(Marisol shakes her head no.)

You're in Brooklyn.
MARISOL *(Empty)*: Wow. I finally made it. I'm here.
LENNY: Everybody comes to this street eventually.
MARISOL: Why?
LENNY: People are buried here. It looks like a sidewalk. But it's
not. It's a tomb.
MARISOL: For who?
LENNY: For babies. *Angelitos.*

*(Lenny removes a slab of sidewalk concrete and starts digging up
the dirt beneath it. There's a tiny wooden box there.)*

The city provides these coffins. There are numbers on them.
The city knows how we live.

(Lenny gently places the baby's body in the box.)

These are babies born on the street. Little girls of the twilight
hours who never felt warm blankets around their bodies.
Never drank their mothers' holy milk. Little boys born with
coke in their blood. This is where babies who die on the street
are taken to rest. You never heard of it?
MARISOL: Never.

(Lenny puts the box in the ground and covers it up with dirt.)

LENNY: Everyone who sleeps and begs in the open air knows this
address. We come with flowers, with crucifixes, with offer-
ings. The wind plays organ music. Hard concrete turns into

gentle moss so the babies can decompose in grace. We all come here sooner or later to pay respects to the most fragile of the street people.

(Lenny replaces the concrete slab and scratches the name of the child into the concrete. He says a prayer. If there are other homeless people onstage, they pick up the prayer and repeat it softly underneath Lenny.)

Matthew, Mark, Luke, and John.
Bless the bed that I lie on.
Four corners to my bed.
Four angels 'round my head.
One to watch and one to pray.
And two to bear your soul away.

(Lenny kisses the ground.)

'Night, little Marisol.

(Lenny lies on the ground and falls asleep. Exhausted, Marisol looks at the tiny cemetery. She reads the names scratched into the sidewalk.)

MARISOL: Fermin Rivera . . . born March 14, died March 16 . . . Jose Amengual . . . born August 2, died August 2 . . . Delfina Perez . . . born December 23, died January 6 . . . Jonathan Sand . . . born July 1, died July 29 . . . Wilfredo Terron . . . dates unknown . . . no name . . . no name . . . no name . . .

(Marisol can't read anymore. She sits in the middle of the child cemetery, exhausted, not able to think, feel, or react anymore. For all she knows, this could be the end of the world.
Marisol lies on the street, in Lenny's arms, and falls asleep.
Upstage there's the sound of marching feet. The Skinhead enters and marches toward the sleeping Marisol and Lenny and stops. Only as the light comes up on the Skinhead do we realize it's June.)

JUNE *(To herself, indicating Marisol)*: Look at this goddamn thing, this waste, this fucking parasite. God, I'm so sick of it. Sick of the eyesore. Sick of the diseases. Sick of the drugs. Sick of the homelessness. Sick of the border babies. Sick of the dark skin. Sick of that compassion thing! That's where it all started! When they put in that fucking compassion thing! *(Furious)* *I mean, why can't they just go AWAY?* I mean, okay, if you people want to kill yourselves, fine, do it: kill yourselves with your crack and your incest and your promiscuity and your homo anal intercourse . . . just leave me to take care of myself and my own. Leave me to my gardens. I'm good in my gardens. I'm good on my acres of green grass. God distributes green grass in just the right way! Take care of your own. Take care of your family. If everybody did that . . . I swear on my gold Citibank MasterCard . . . there wouldn't be any problems, anywhere, in the next millennium . . .

(June looks down at Marisol. She unscrews the can of gasoline and starts pouring gasoline on Marisol and Lenny. Marisol wakes up. June strikes a match. Marisol jumps at June, grabbing her.)

MARISOL: Cut that shit out you fucking Nazi!

(June tries to throw the match on Marisol.)

JUNE: Stay still so I can burn you!

(Marisol grabs June and tries to push her away from Lenny. They're face-to-face for the first time.)

What a day I'm having, huh?
MARISOL *(Startled)*: . . . June?
JUNE: I started out burning hobos and ended up torching half the city! The entire Upper West Side up in ashes!
MARISOL *(Overjoyed)*: Oh God, I found you.
JUNE: You got anything for me?!
MARISOL: I thought Lenny killed you—

JUNE: You got nothing for me? Get outta my way, asshole!

MARISOL: Don't you remember me?

JUNE: You should see what I did! It's fire on a massive scale! Buildings melted all down! Consumed! Ashes of those evaporated dreams are all over the fucking place!

MARISOL: June—it's Marisol . . .

(Marisol throws both arms around June, embraces her tightly, and kisses her. June tries to escape.)

JUNE: We could be picked up real fast by the police . . . they've built great big facilities for us . . . 'cause our numbers are swelling . . .

(Marisol tries to hold June. June resists. But the prolonged and violent contact with Marisol's body has started to awaken June's memory. She begins to sound a little like her old self.)

But they won't take me! I have a strategy now! I burn bag people! The troop likes that!

MARISOL: No more! That's not you!

(Marisol throws the can of gasoline into the trash bin. She grabs June's hand and pulls June toward Lenny. June resists.)

JUNE: The Citicorp building was a great place to hide. A man would pull your teeth for free in Port Authority—

MARISOL: Lenny's right here . . .

JUNE: I hear the water in the Central Park reservoir is salty 'cause angels are falling outta the sky, Marisol . . .

MARISOL *(Astonished)*: You said my name. You said Marisol.

(Marisol joyfully embraces June and kisses her. That pushes June over the edge and she collapses. Marisol catches her and lays her gently on the ground. Marisol sits with June's head on her lap. This time June does not resist.)

JUNE *(Weak, rubbing her head)*: I can't understand these nightmares I'm having . . .

(Marisol holds June. June and Lenny quietly start to cry.)

MARISOL: We survived. We survived, June.

(Marisol looks around her—at her two crippled, sobbing friends—at the distorted world—all too aware of the graveyard that has become the site of their reunion.)

For what? To do what?

(Marisol looks up at the crown—a long, still moment.)

Fuck you. Just *fuck you*!

(Loud machine-gun fire rips the air. Marisol hits the ground and covers June and Lenny with her body.)

June, Lenny . . . don't you guys worry . . . I have a clear vision for us. I know what I want to do.

(The machine-gun firing stops. Marisol kisses her friends.)

Listen to me. We're going to find the angels. And I'm going to ask them to touch your foreheads. To press their angelic fingers into your temples. Fire your minds with instant light. Blow up your bad dreams. And resurrect you.

(Marisol looks up at the crown.)

And then we're going to join them. Then we're going to fight with the angels.

(Marisol helps June and Lenny to their feet. June and Lenny see each other and embrace.)

LENNY *(To June)*: I'm sorry for everything I did . . .
JUNE *(To Lenny, kissing him)*: I'm sorry, too, Lenny . . .

(As Marisol takes their hands to start their new journey, the Woman With Furs enters, unseen, behind them. She is completely still. She is holding an Uzi.)

MARISOL: What a time to be alive, huh? On one hand, we're nothing. We're dirt. On the other hand, we're the reason the universe was made.

(The Woman With Furs loads the Uzi. Bombs are heard.)

JUNE: What's that noise?
MARISOL: Right now, thousands upon millions of angels are dying on our behalf. Isn't that amazing? The silver cities of Heaven are burning for us. Attacks and counterattacks are ruining galaxies. The ripped-up planets are making travel impossible. And triumphant angels are taking over the television stations. All for us. All for me.

(The Woman With Furs points the Uzi at Marisol, June, and Lenny.)

WOMAN WITH FURS: Sorry, Marisol. We don't need revolution here. We can't have upheaval at the drop of a hat. No demonstrations here! No putting up pamphlets! No shoving daisies into the rifles of militiamen! No stopping tanks by standing in their way!

(Marisol turns to look at the Woman With Furs.)

MARISOL: . . . Unless you want to join us—?
WOMAN WITH FURS: Traitors! Credit risks!

(Marisol goes to the Woman With Furs and the Woman With Furs blasts Marisol, pumping hundreds of rounds into her. She dies instantly and falls to the ground. The Woman With Furs exits.)

There's a blackout.
Suddenly, the stage is bathed in strange light. We hear the strange, indecipherable sounds of the angelic war.
June and Lenny kneel where Marisol has fallen. Marisol is standing apart, alone, in her own light. Marisol's voice is slightly amplified:)

MARISOL: I'm killed instantly. Little blazing lead meteors enter my body. My blood cells ride those bullets into outer space. My soul surges up the oceans of the Milky Way at the speed of light. At the moment of death, I see the invisible war.

(Beautiful music.
The stage goes black, except for a light on Marisol.)

Thousands of years of fighting pass in an instant. New and terrible forms of warfare, monstrous weapons, and unimagined strains of terror are created and destroyed in billionths of a second. Galaxies spring from a single drop of angel's sweat while hundreds of armies fight and die on the fingertips of children in the Bronx.

(Light upstage reveals the Angel. She's dressed in a filthy, tattered uniform: the war has ravaged her. She also has huge magnificent wings: her wings of war. She's got an Uzi machine gun.
The Angel fires her Uzi into the air, at the invisible legions of God's loyal warriors. The terrible sounds of war.
The angelic vision lasts only seconds. The stage once again goes to black. A spotlight on Marisol.)

Three hundred million million beautiful angels die in the first charge of the Final Battle. The oceans are salty with rebel blood. Angels drop like lightning from the dying sky. The rebels are in full retreat. There's chaos. There's blood and fire and ambulances and Heaven's soldiers scream and fight and die in beautiful, beautiful light. It looks like the revolution is doomed . . .

(Light upstage reveals a single homeless person angrily throwing rocks at the sky. The homeless person is joined by Lenny and June.)

. . . then, as if one body, one mind, the innocent of the earth take to the streets with anything they can find—rocks, sticks, screams—and aim their displeasure at the senile sky and fire into the tattered wind on the side of the angels . . . billions of poor, of homeless, of peaceful, of silent, of angry . . . fighting and fighting as no species has ever fought before. Inspired by the earthly noise, the rebels advance!

(A small moon appears in the sky, far, far away.)

New ideas rip the Heavens. New powers are created. New miracles are signed into law. It's the first day of the new history . . .

(There's a few seconds of tremendous noise as the war hits its climax.
Then silence.
The Angel appears next to Marisol, wingless, unarmed, holding the gold crown in her hands. The Angel holds the crown out to the audience as Marisol looks at her.)

Oh God. What light. What possibilities. What hope.

(The Angel kisses Marisol.
Bright, bright light begins to shine directly into the audience's eyes—for several seconds—and Marisol, the Angel, June, Lenny, and the homeless people seem to be turned into light. Then, all seem to disappear in the wild light of the new millennium— blackout.)

EACH DAY DIES
WITH SLEEP

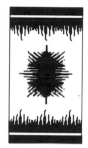

For Wilfredo Terrón, Ramon Rivera
and Rosemary Rivera

". . . because even the tiny banquet of a spider
is enough to upset the entire equilibrium of the sky."

—*Federico García Lorca*

Each Day Dies with Sleep received its world premiere in a co-production by Circle Repertory Company (Tanya Berezin, Artistic Director) and Berkeley Repertory Theatre (Sharon Ott, Artistic Director) on April 10, 1990. It was directed by Roberta Levitow; the set design was by Tom Kamm; the costume design was by Tina Cantu Navarro; the lighting design was by Robert Wierzel; the sound design was by Barney Jones (Berkeley) and Janet Kalas (New York); the scenic projections were designed by Charles Rose; the props were designed by Skip Epperson; original music was by Rebeca Mauleon and Joe Taylor; the dramaturgs were Mame Hunt (Berkeley) and Adrienne Heigel (New York); and the stage managers were Meryl Lind Shaw (Berkeley) and Fred Reinglas (New York). The cast was as follows:

AUGIE	Alex Colón
NELLY	Erica Gimpel
JOHNNY	Randy Vasquez

The premiere of the play was made possible, in part, with a grant from the Rockefeller Foundation and with public funds from the National Endowment for the Arts, the New York State Council on the Arts and the New York City Department of Cultural Affairs. The premiere was also a part of the "AT&T New Plays for the Nineties Project."

CHARACTERS

AUGIE, her father, in his forties.
NELLY, a woman in her twenties.
JOHNNY, her husband, in his thirties.

PLACE

Nelly's home on the East Coast
and Nelly's home in Los Angeles.

TIME

The present. The play covers several years.

ACT ONE

Scene One

Three playing areas: a furnished room center, flanked by two small empty areas. There's a door in the center area and one in the small area left. There's an engine block in the area right. All areas are dark. Lively guitar music is heard. An image of an orange tree is projected on a wall.

Lights up center. There are strangely shaped windows, a dusty, beat-up old couch and worn, overstuffed chairs in this room. Everything looks a hundred years old. Nelly, early twenties, is sitting on the floor in the center room, surrounded by a mountain of freshly cleaned socks. There are hundreds of socks. Nelly is trying to find matching pairs. She's in desperate need of sleep. By her side is a toy truck which she periodically plays with like a spastic child.

Feeling hungry, Nelly goes to the sofa. She's hidden some food under the cushions. She finds her food and eats fast. She notices the image of the orange tree. She giggles. She claps her hands and the image changes: we see the Pacific Ocean. This makes her so happy, she laughs.

A gunshot is heard offstage. The images disappear.

Nelly's father, Augie, enters, dodging the shot we just heard. Augie is a robust Latino in his late forties.

Johnny appears, playing the guitar. He's a handsome, beautifully built man, early thirties. He watches this scene, unnoticed.

AUGIE *(Whispers to Nelly)*: What's wrong with those animals? Why are they shooting at their own father? *(Shouting to ceiling)* You kids better get to bed! Stop shooting guns or I'll come up there with my belt!

(Guitar music stops. We hear hundreds of footsteps as an army of children run to their bedrooms. Dozens of doors are slammed.
Silence. Augie smiles triumphantly. Nelly's too afraid to look at him.
Note: in the first two scenes, Nelly has trouble speaking, as if her mouth were unable to keep up with her rapid mind. Her vocal rhythm, volume or speed are always off. It's a struggle.)

NELLY: It's three o'clock! In the morning! What'd you expect—a hero's welcome?
AUGIE: . . . And lucky me gets to come home to the pinhead.

(Augie staggers toward the offstage bedroom. He opens the door, starts to exit, but is repulsed by an incredible smell coming from the room.)

How can I sleep in there? Your mother smells like a forest of dead animals. Is it any wonder I go PARTYING?

(He reenters the center room. Frightened, Nelly springs to her feet and runs around on all fours. Walking on all fours is the only way she can get around.)

NELLY: Do not come near me! Go away!
AUGIE: And what're the little assassins doing up? And on a school night? Huh, Pinhead?
NELLY: I am not Pinhead! Say my *real* name, Dad—
AUGIE: Not *homework*, right? My offshoots aren't up there doing their *homework*. They're up there *plotting*. Making secret plans to waste me. Well it's not going to work. I'm too smart.

(Augie pours himself a drink. Nelly glares at him.)

NELLY *(Sarcastic)*: Have a drink.
AUGIE: Don't sass me, Pinhead.

(Before he drinks, Augie takes out a deck of tarot cards. He flips them over, studying them carefully, looking for omens. Nelly looks at Augie angrily and holds out her hand.)

NELLY: Hey! *So where's my birthday present?*
AUGIE *(Flipping cards)*: Sorry, Pinhead, I decided tonight: *no more celebrating birthdays.* I can't remember twenty-one birthdays. And your mother won't get her heaving bulk out of bed to help me. So from now on, we celebrate *one* birthday, *my* birthday, a day we can all rejoice in, like the birth of Jesus.

(Disappointed, Nelly plays with the truck to keep from crying.)

Taste this for me. The cards look ominous.

(Nelly tastes drink. She's gripped by convulsions. She trembles horribly and falls over dead.)

One passionate night, I swear, I'm gonna launch a preemptive strike and erase *all* you kids from the world. Then I'll start over *fresh*, with a sexy young wife, and twenty-one new children *who will love me.*

(Nelly dog-walks offstage.)

NELLY *(Off)*: Maybe this time? You'll remember their names?

(Augie starts undressing for bed. He strips down to his shorts.)

AUGIE: I can still make babies, you know. Don't question that. I can get *trees* pregnant. I'm a one-man human reforestation program.

(Nelly comes back on with a bucket of warm water. She sniffs Augie's fingers.)

NELLY: Your fingers smell like *two* women. Girls! Young! Stupid!

AUGIE *(Laughs)*: Yeah, they were very young all right. And very stupid.

NELLY: Oh go clean up! I smell adultery in your pores and I'm gagging!

AUGIE: Aw, leave me alone, my day sucked. It all started this morning with the sound of Raphael's screams as Sylvia whaled on his face with a crescent wrench. Then it was Hector's screams 'cause he's drowning in the blood of Raphael's massive nosebleed and would have died if I hadn't performed mouth-to-mouth CPR on him. Then the assassination attempts started. Floating like an oil slick in my coffee was Liquid Drano. I was in the tub? And one of your doomed siblings dropped a live radio in the water. Sizzled the hair off my legs! All that before breakfast! At lunch, Rosaline sets Anita's cat on fire and the cat's running around the house, its organs bubbling and eyes sizzling, and Roberto's brought home by the cops in handcuffs for extorting money in school from the first graders, and Marcus Junior's got an olive pit so far up his nose it's playing pinball with his goddamn brains! And this social worker's got the brass balls to say the way out of my poverty is sterilization—"I will not be sterilized!"—I said, as I threw her through a window on the second floor.

(Nelly dries Augie's feet. Contented, Augie lies on the couch, his bed for the night. Nelly jumps on his stomach like a heavy cat. Augie groans.)

NELLY: My name? My name? Remember my name?

AUGIE: Why're you always *at* me about your goddamn name? I draw a blank on your name.

NELLY: Notice? You have twenty-one children. I'm the *only* one staying up late, making sure you're not homecoming stabbed in the heart. Only me! I care!

AUGIE: Yeah. Why is that? You want something? An allowance?

NELLY: Yes! To hear my *name*!

AUGIE: I forgot it.

NELLY: It's Nelly . . . *Nelly* . . . you sad big fool!

(Nelly jumps off Augie and sits on the floor. She plays with the truck and cries quietly.)

AUGIE: Awwwwwwww. Are you pouting? Don't you get enough love?

NELLY *(Pointing to herself)*: I'm a slave. Workhorse. Sock cleaner. Cook. And I am not sleeping well! Not slept since the last full moon: I'm the janitor for twenty brothers and sisters.

AUGIE *(Laughing)*: Hey. Can't blame me for all those kids. I haven't touched your mother in years. The sun gets her pregnant. Cockroaches and clouds get her pregnant: the *horny moon*. That's why your brothers and sisters are so friggin' weird. And I swear her pregnancies are getting shorter and shorter all the time!

(Nelly tries to stand up. It takes great effort and she almost succeeds. Augie watches her struggle, frightened. Her speech is almost "normal.")

NELLY: Don't turn around too fast, Dad—don't blink too hard—or you'll see me gone.

AUGIE *(Alarmed)*: Are you going to leave me, Pinhead?

NELLY: I daydreamed about California! California sun!

AUGIE: Quit saying that! I'm your father! Show some respect!

NELLY: You're not my father 'til you remember my name! Drunk old pig!

(Augie lunges at Nelly. She screams and runs on all fours, throwing socks at him. Augie is too drunk and tired to chase her. He fixes another drink.

There's a loud groaning noise offstage, like wood scraping against wood.)

AUGIE *(Frightened by the noise)*: What's that? That the house? Is it my imagination or is this house getting *bigger*? I'm walking up the driveway tonight, looking up and up and up . . . and there are new *windows* up there.

NELLY: The house is an organism. Reproducing like you do. Like children and rooms are unimportant and don't need to be cared for.

(Augie laughs, scared.)

AUGIE: If I care for one of you, I have to care for all of you, and who's got that much time?

NELLY *(On the attack)*: The house is like you. Full of lies. Sick dreams. I don't know the real number of rooms: there's the television room, the sex room, the room of endless hunger, the room of storms, the room of teardrops, the rooms of moss and mushrooms. There are animals all over the house! They're just cubs now. Just baby carnivores. But they will grow. I don't want to be around then! No thanks to cleaning animal shit all my life!

(Augie looks at her.)

AUGIE: It's Alicia! Your name is Alicia!

(Johnny strums the guitar. Augie grabs Nelly around the waist, makes her stand upright and dances with her as Johnny plays. Nelly tries to squirm free, but can't.)

Sleep with me.

NELLY *(Shocked)*: I'm your daughter.

AUGIE: I don't know that. There are so many people living here who I don't know, you could be the new social worker or something . . .

(Augie laughs drunkenly and continues dancing as Nelly continues to squirm. Augie smiles at a recent memory.)

I was on the dance floor tonight. A girl's tongue was in my ear, tickling the loose nerves in my brain. She scrambled my memories until I didn't know who I was anymore. It was great.

(A woman screams, offstage. Augie and Nelly look at each other.)

NELLY: There's no avoiding her. The mammoth woman can smell your nasty fingertips.

(Augie falls asleep in Nelly's arms. Johnny continues playing. Augie dances in his sleep as Nelly pulls him toward the area left. She opens the door and pushes him into the offstage bedroom. She closes the door.

  Exhausted, Nelly goes to the center room and tries to sleep on the sofa, but can't. We see projections of dreamlike black and white clouds. Lights suggest the passage of time.)

Scene Two

As Nelly tosses and turns, Johnny gets down on his belly and crawls across the floor, commando-style, toward the area right. The face of a pretty young woman, with the word "Gloria" over it, is projected. Nelly sees Johnny and jumps on his back, squashing him. She laughs.

NELLY: You've got teflon balls, little horsie! Big metal balls!
JOHNNY: Get off my back, Nelly!
NELLY: Where're you going? Upstairs? At five o'clock in the morning, Johnny??
JOHNNY: Felicia's room—
NELLY: *Felicia's!?* You dumped Lizbeth so soon?! *(Hitting him)* Slime! Disease! Pestilence!

(Nelly goes to Augie's door and pounds on it.)

Hey Dad! Wake up!

(Johnny grabs Nelly and pulls her away from the door. They struggle violently.)

JOHNNY: Hey! I don't want that son of a bitch to see me!

(Johnny pins her down. He's on top of her. They look at each other. Johnny tries to kiss her. She pushes his mouth away.)

NELLY: Yuck! Your spit tastes like gasoline!

(She bites him on the arm. He yowls and jumps off her, rubbing his arm in pain.)

JOHNNY: So? Okay, I love you. Those weird-color eyes of yours make me nuts. Admit you love me too.
NELLY: Admit all your bastards. Felicia's three kids! Maritza's twins! Nilda's retarded son! They are yours!
JOHNNY: Will you slow *down*? You think too fast for your mouth—
NELLY: My nieces and nephews are all your babies—
JOHNNY: Oh man. That's beat. That's just a rumor.
NELLY: The bastards play guitar. Flex muscles. Comb hair. Like you do.
JOHNNY *(Combing hair)*: Coincidence.

(He smiles at her. She scampers away. He follows.)

Awwww, just admit you love me, Nelly, *c'mon.*
NELLY: Oh. Go to Felicia. I don't care.
JOHNNY: I can skip Felicia. I always thought you were prettier. I just thought you were too young and weird—
NELLY: It's my birthday tonight! I got no presents!
JOHNNY: I'm your present. I know you look at me. A guy can tell. You're not the pinhead everyone says.
NELLY: I am not stupid!

JOHNNY: And you get me riled up the way you crawl around on all fours and misuse your pronouns. Do you think I'm good-looking? Do you?

NELLY *(Soft)*: Maybe. Confused. Don't trust you.

(Johnny comes toward Nelly again, but she runs away, pointing at the projection.)

No! You love Gloria.

JOHNNY: Gloria? No! She's a, she's a *girl.* Sixteen. A stick.

NELLY: You're killing time—you're waiting for puberty to explode her—then you'll pounce her bones and forget me.

JOHNNY: I've been waiting for *you!* To walk and talk right. I see improvement. I know just being with me is making you better all the time. *(He tries to touch her)* Nelly, Nelly, I play guitar like the wind.

(Nelly stands completely straight for the first time in the play. It's a struggle. He looks at her extremely surprised.)

NELLY: You hurt Maritza, then Nilda, then Lizbeth, then Felicia. That's a disgusting track record!

JOHNNY: But don't you think I'm beautiful?

(She's back on all fours. She plays with the truck, ignoring him, which he can't stand.)

You're right. I made it with all your big sisters. I knocked them all up. What can I say? I love this family.

(Nelly turns away disgusted.)

I can't help what nature's done to me. It's some magic I got. I'm a victim. I'm too beautiful to live.

(Johnny grabs her, holding her still.)

You make me feel different than your sisters do. I never met a woman who could resist me. How can you do that? How come you're the only one? You know how crazy that makes me get?

(He tries to kiss her; she pulls away, still standing.)

NELLY: I will not be your next casualty, Johnny Amengual.
JOHNNY: Boy, your syntax has really picked up.
NELLY: If Nelly and Johnny . . . *exist* . . . the buck stops here. We stay together. There's no Gloria after me. I am forever or nothing.
JOHNNY: That's a long time.
NELLY: Not worth it? Think about this.

(Nelly kisses him viciously. Then she pushes him away roughly. The kiss stuns Johnny.)

That's so—you know what—you give up—if you hurt me.

(She kisses him again. She is tender. She pushes him away tenderly.)

That's. A memory of me. Burned in your skin. Your nerves will haunt you with that memory, drive you to a crazy suicide—and blast you—to a million, lovesick stars.

(Nelly crawls to the socks. Johnny is reeling from her kiss.)

JOHNNY: What'd you do to my mouth? WHAT WAS THAT? That wasn't human, Nelly.
NELLY: Magic? Me?
JOHNNY: I've never—in my whole life—tasted—who knew you could do that?!
NELLY *(Dismissing him)*: Felicia? Waiting?
JOHNNY: How can I kiss Felicia after this? You ruined me!
NELLY *(Pointing to projection)*: Gloria? Bitch?
JOHNNY: Gloria who? Nelly, let's get married, tonight, please, we gotta.

(Nelly laughs.)

Hey, this isn't easy for me, so don't laugh! But the truth is, I'm getting too old for this. Breaking into your father's castle, slithering up endless flights of stairs, through gloomy bedrooms and weird animals. I need you to help me grow up, like I'm helping you talk.

(Johnny kisses Nelly. She continues working on the socks, unfazed.)

C'mon, what do you want from me?

NELLY: Employment history. I want to know your prospects.

JOHNNY: My what?

NELLY: Johnny. I'm the—middle—child of twenty-one children—number eleven. *I haven't left this house in two years.* I want no more of that! I have to know what I'm getting into with you. I want prospects. I want better.

JOHNNY: I have prospects. I'm going to quit working on cars and make money on my knockout looks. Be a fashion model.

NELLY: Be serious!

(She angrily grabs him by the lapels and shakes him.)

I have serious ideas! Ideas are bursting my skull open! I want to *make* something. I don't want to watch and worry over brothers and sisters the rest of a—short—life.

JOHNNY: Like what ideas?

NELLY: My plan is this: I can fall asleep and dream winning lottery numbers. I can win big bucks real fast.

JOHNNY: You can?

NELLY: Make big bucks. Move to California. Away from Dad. Open a garage. Fix Porsches, Mercedes, Jaguars. You and me. We'll be a team and we'll be rich, Johnny.

JOHNNY: But fixing cars is so *boring* . . .

NELLY: I *want* boring. There's too much excitement in my life. I don't want any more violence, hunger, and screaming babies. I want to sleep eight hours a day. Every day of the week.

Johnny. *(She touches his face tenderly)* You're thirty-five years old. You're still living with your Mami. You don't have the drive. I have the drive. *I want to go.* Go together?

JOHNNY: Are you using me?

(Nelly enthusiastically nods yes.)

Oh. But you can walk out of here without me. You don't need me.

NELLY: *I do!* Do you notice something? My brothers and sisters never leave the house. Why? My father's tyrant blood is in us. His blood controls us. Keeps us afraid.

JOHNNY: I'm not afraid of him.

NELLY: I know! Your hate for him is in my blood now. It's going to help me escape him.

(Nelly kisses Johnny. The projection of Gloria disappears. Nelly smiles.)

Want you. Marry you.

JOHNNY: No. "I want to marry you." Say it.

NELLY: "I want to marry you."

JOHNNY: I want to marry you. I want to have sex with you first.

NELLY: I can't sex here. I have no bedroom here.

(We see projections of children sleeping two and three to a bed.)

Every night, I wander. From room to room. Looking for pieces of the floor not covered by members of my big family or animal droppings. But even in this house, with its hundred rooms, I share space with somebody. If I *do* fall asleep, I can't rest. My different-color eyes are always in conflict and they keep me awake. *(She stands up and walks normally, though with some effort. Her speech is nearly flawless)* The blue eye hates the gray eye for something the gray eye did to the blue eye when I was still a fetus floating like a little fish in my mother's huge body. Floating there among the schools of unborn brothers and sisters. Today, the fighting between my eyes gives me headaches, Johnny, and prophetic dreams. *(She smiles at him)* Help me rest. I'll stop using you. I'll love you—fiercely—for the rest of my life.

JOHNNY: I think you're beautiful. Do you think I'm beautiful?

NELLY: Right now? I think you're very, very . . .

(Nelly falls asleep. Johnny lifts her and starts to carry her offstage. As he approaches the exit, the projection of Gloria comes back on. Johnny stops to look at the beautiful Gloria.)

Scene Three

It's morning. Johnny is holding Nelly. Augie enters the center room wearing party clothes. Johnny sees Augie and quickly puts Nelly down. She sleeps standing up. Frightened, Johnny crawls out of the house.

Nelly is seized by violent dreams as the projections of the black and white clouds return. She twists and shakes as the following are also rapidly projected: Augie in a wheelchair, Johnny wearing a white mask, a severed hand, a burning car, a burning house.

Augie—hung over, brittle—goes to Nelly and shakes her. She wakes up. The projections disappear. From this point on, Nelly walks and speaks normally. She looks at Augie a moment, getting her courage up.

NELLY: I'm going to California with Johnny Amengual. And you can't stop me.

(Nelly starts throwing the socks offstage and into the audience. She dances happily around the stage, a free woman. The orange tree is projected on the wall.)

AUGIE: What are you doing upright?

NELLY: Blame Johnny.

AUGIE: And speaking sequentially? Is this a joke?

NELLY: I'm a fast learner.

AUGIE: Then learn me some breakfast and clean socks, Pinhead.
I have a party to go to. I need to be fresh.

NELLY: No more socks! I have found life outside of socks and hard
labor!

AUGIE: I don't like this new turn of events here.

NELLY: From now on my life will be filled with transmissions, bat-
teries, windshields, flat tires, and money, money, money.

*(Nelly starts to leave. Augie claps his hands and Nelly freezes in
her tracks.)*

AUGIE: You going to California? With Johnny Amengual? Felicia's
boyfriend?

NELLY: My fiancé.

AUGIE: Why? A man finally looks at you and you think it's love?

NELLY: He's kind.

AUGIE: Do you know how many of your nieces and nephews are
his children?

NELLY: He hates you. He gives me strength.

AUGIE: No man should be that pretty. I hate that face of his. It
drives me crazy those perfect bones, those dog eyes—

NELLY: I'm going—

AUGIE *(Laughs)*: And I thought you were the smart one of the
family!

NELLY: Liar. You never thought of me as anything. I never crossed
that sick cesspool frontier you call a *mind*, Dad. Let me stay
anonymous. Let Lizbeth and Maritza take care of you, I'm
out. *(She tries to leave)*

AUGIE: Another step. And I'll smack your face across the goddamn room. *(Takes off his belt)* Then I'll get rough.

(Nelly stops. She knows the threat is real.)

NELLY: I'm not just me. I'm two people.

AUGIE: The pinhead can walk and talk and think. Well, golly.
(Laughs. Puts belt on) I couldn't stop your idiot sisters from
falling for Johnny Amengual. Guess I can't stop you.

NELLY *(A chant)*: I am Johnny. Johnny is me. I am Johnny—

AUGIE: But if you're going to get married, you're going to follow family *tradition*. You and Johnny will move in, take the top floor, and raise your big family in my house.

NELLY: Why do you want to do that to me?

AUGIE: You don't love Johnny.

NELLY: You don't know me.

AUGIE: I can see it in your eye. Your left eye. The gray one. The one I gave you. It's saying: you're only using him and you know he's going to run to Gloria the day she turns legal.

NELLY: I don't think so. I don't think I'm so easy to read anymore.

(Nelly starts to go again. Augie grabs her, suddenly very afraid.)

AUGIE: If you go, who's going to taste my coffee and make sure there's no Drano in it? Huh?!

NELLY: Dad—

AUGIE: And you can't leave me alone with your mother. She's a cannibal. She's been trying to swallow me. You know her appetite. I'm going with you to California.

NELLY: I'm going out that door to run across the street to Johnny's car. Try and follow me, Dad.

AUGIE: I'll be right behind you.

NELLY: Do it. You're not going to make it to the other side. I saw it in a dream. You're going to get hit by a car.

AUGIE: Liar.

NELLY: Look in my left eye and tell me I'm lying.

(Augie looks in her eye. We and Augie see the projection of Augie in the wheelchair, a broken man.)

AUGIE: That's—that's—

NELLY *(Quickly kisses him)*: Goodbye. *(She runs off)*

AUGIE: That's—that's a *lie!*

(Augie runs after her. We see a projection of a car coming down a busy street.)

NELLY *(Offstage)*: Follow me! Follow me, Dad! Follow meeeeeeeeee!

(We hear Augie scream and see a projection of a close-up of Augie's contorted face. A trickle of blood forms where Augie's mouth is, and runs down, bright red, the length of the projection screen.)

Scene Four

The projection of Augie fades out. Nelly enters. She sadly wipes the blood from the screen with a sponge. She exits. Lights down on all the rooms.

Scene Five

Lights up on the left area of the stage. Nelly enters, pushing Augie in a wheelchair. Augie is paralyzed from the waist down. He wears battered pajamas. On his lap is a small radio, a yo-yo, a telephone, a shaving basin, a razor and shaving cream. His eyes, though still bright, are now full of fear and confusion.

A spotlight reveals Johnny, in the right area of the stage, now a garage. Johnny is dressed as a mechanic, working on the car engine.

The center room remains dark. We hear dozens of feet running around. Then dozens of cars being started. They all drive away until there's silence.

Nelly shaves Augie.

NELLY: I talked to Mom. She, uh, didn't want you sleeping in the same bed as her. She says looking at you gets her depressed. *(Beat)* And I can't stay anymore.

(Augie violently shakes his head back and forth.)

Dad! Johnny's in Los Angeles waiting for me. He opened a garage and bought a pretty little house on Laurel Canyon Boulevard with our lottery money.

(In the center room, in the dark, Johnny puts up an orange tree. During the following Johnny also fills the center room with new furniture.)

He says "Nelly and Johnny's" is doing great. Hired two men to work under him. And he never talks about modeling. He's growing up. Says he misses me.

(Augie starts to cry.)

It's going to be fine here. Mom's going to be a different woman. She's going to get out of bed and exercise. Do toe touches and leg lifts. And she says she's going to spend every penny of the insurance money on your comfort. Blow your nose.

(Nelly holds a handkerchief for Augie. He blows his nose.)

You have to trust her. There's no one else. The kids and grandkids have left. The spell you had on their blood is broken. They've dispersed all over the world and left no forwarding addresses.

(Augie starts to cry.)

Dad! This is no time to get sentimental about children you never cared about. Stop it or I leave.

(Augie stops crying.)

One more thing. Your children left their pets behind. There are bears and monkeys and snakes and wild dogs living in the house. They're a little hungry. But don't worry. Mom's going to keep this door locked. *(She plugs the telephone into the wall)* I have a lot to do in California. I have to make up for all those years gibbering like an idiot and running around like a dog. I've got a five-year plan. *(She demonstrates the yo-yo)* See? Isn't this fun?

(Johnny looks at her across the distance of three thousand miles.)

JOHNNY: Forget him. We have things to do, babe.
NELLY: I have to go.

(Johnny exits. Nelly kisses Augie and exits. Augie's wife's laughter is heard offstage. The laughter reaches a peak—Augie covers his ears—then stops. Lights down on Augie.)

Scene Six

Lights up on center room, now Nelly and Johnny's living room in Los Angeles. Lots of sunshine streams in through the windows. Growing out of the floor is the orange tree, heavy with ripe oranges. The roots of the tree extend the length and breadth of the room. Johnny runs on, chased by Nelly, who is shaking up a bottle of champagne. She sprays champagne all over Johnny.

NELLY: To our one-thousandth repair! Woooooooooooooo-ooooooo-eeeeee!
JOHNNY: Whoooooooooo-ooooooooooo-eeeeeeeeee!!
NELLY *(Drinking)*: Whooooooooo-eeeeeeeeeee-he-he-he-he!!

(Nelly hands Johnny the bottle of champagne and he drinks from it.)

JOHNNY: Have you had one of these oranges? They're incredible. *(He picks an orange from the tree, slices it in half and eats it)* Hhmmmmmmmmmm. They're *intoxicating*.

(Nelly eats an orange. She reacts as if electricity has shot through her.)

NELLY: Hmmmmmmmmmmmmmmmmmm. They make you dizzy!
JOHNNY: Hmmmmmmmmmmmmmmmmmmm.
NELLY *(Intoxicated)*: California is clean. And bright. And modern. And sleek. And do you think everyone in Los Angeles has an orange tree growing out of their living room floor . . . ?

JOHNNY: I got it! I'll strip to my shorts. I'll put on a blindfold. I'll play the guitar . . .

NELLY: In the middle of the afternoon?

JOHNNY: . . . you can sneak up on me, throw me on the floor, and put that delirious tongue of yours to work.

NELLY: But we have work to do, beautiful. Money to make.

JOHNNY: Give it a break, Nelly. How about this? You tie me to the hood of the red T-bird and lick me till I'm senseless.

NELLY: Hmmmmm, that sounds like fun . . .

JOHNNY: You know what's fun? Pour the orange juice on your skin. The feeling is incredible.

(Nelly squeezes an orange on her hand.)

NELLY: Wow. Hmmmmmmmmmmmmmmmm!

JOHNNY: You feel every little thing about three hundred percent more.

NELLY *(Smiles at him)*: You're a wizard, Johnny, the way you make me feel.

(Johnny cuts open another orange and rubs the juice on Nelly's neck and back. She closes her eyes, relishing it.)

Oh God. I feel like candy.

(She kisses him. Lights down on them.)

Scene Seven

Lights up on Augie, who is now sitting in a wheelchair with square wheels. He looks terrible. His wife's laughter is coming from the offstage bedroom. Augie bangs on the door with an old broom.

AUGIE: CUT IT OUT! I'm not going to sit here and quietly decompose while you and your boyfriend sin against God and nature. *(He bangs on the door with the broom)* A woman your age! Mother of twenty-one children! Have some respect for the sacred vows we took, will ya?! *(He pounds on the door and the laughter subsides)* Think you're twenty-one years old again? Huh? Think you still have something to give a man? Huhn? What do you have? A couple of moldy orgasms? Just tell your boyfriend you went to school with his grandmother! We'll see his enthusiasm drop then, won't we? His enthusiasm will look pretty flaccid then, huh? *(He bangs on the wall)* GIVE ME BACK MY OLD WHEELCHAIR. I promise I won't try to escape again. *(He waits for an answer. The silence makes him panic.)* And why don't I hear my children and grandchildren walking around? Where are my babies? Why did they leave me? I wasn't so bad to them! All I hear are the groans of bears and the screams of wild monkeys. Has anybody fed those animals? I know they can smell me and they know I'm defenseless. Okay—tell my children I'll reinstate birthdays! Happy birthday to all them snotnoses! *(He bangs on the wall)* And I've learned my lesson! I had an epiphany! Biggest friggin' epiphany you ever saw! I'm a better man now! I'll never be the way I was! And, oh yeah, I think I want to *EAT* this week, okay?! And someone has to come here and kill the mold that's growing on my arms.

(A spotlight on Nelly asleep on the couch.)

And I want to know where what's-her-name is. My daughter. The only child in this zoo that treated me with due respect. She was here once. She opened windows for me. And sweet air swept into the room with busy fingers cleaning the filth from my skin . . . and hot sunlight cooked every last cold corner of this room and blasted the night to pieces . . . it was great! I saw little pieces of night, shrieking and squeaking and scrambling under all the furniture and hiding in all the cracks of the floor, because of her.

(Augie dials the phone. It rings in Nelly's house. She wakes up. She looks at the phone. Shaking with fear, she just looks at it, not moving. Augie waits, then slams down the phone.)

I can bring her back! All I have to do is remember her name.
I know all their names. I can name all my kids. Oscar,
Maritza, Nilda, Heriberto, Carlos, Marcos, Beto, Lizbeth,
Jesus, Felicia, Che, Gloria, Antonio, Anita, Rosaline,
Primitivo, Ping, Sylvia, Linda, and Freddie. *(Counts on his
fingers)* That's twenty. Oscar, Maritza, Nilda, Heriberto,
Carlos, Marcos, Beto, Lizbeth, Jesus, Felicia, Che, Gloria,
Antonio, Anita, Rosaline, Primitivo, Ping, Sylvia, Linda,
Freddie and, and, and . . . *who?* Goddammit, tell me, who is
she?! Her smell stained the air in this room, making it blue
and gray, like her two-color eyes! My precious girl . . . old
what's-her-damn-friggin'-name . . .

*(He looks around sadly. Nelly looks at the phone. Johnny enters
and stands behind her.)*

JOHNNY: I don't want him bothering you.
NELLY: Go to bed. I'll be fine.

*(Johnny remains, watching the action. Nelly looks at Augie and
calls out softly.)*

Hey! Dad!

*(Augie looks around for the source of Nelly's voice. Frightened, he
hangs on the wall as Nelly watches.)*

AUGIE: Hey! I want to make babies with you! I know your body
can still make babies. *(Grimacing)* That beautiful body I love
so much. *(He waits. No response)* Think I can't do it? Think
I'm dead from the waist down? Well, it still works. It's still in
good working order. *(He looks at his lap in amazement)* Yes it
is. It's working again! Hurry up, take advantage of this, it's
not going to last all night!

*(With incredible effort, Augie tries to push himself to his feet. It
takes a long time. Nelly watches, spellbound.)*

NELLY: I put him in that chair. And Mom's not taking care of him.

JOHNNY: I want you to ravage me tonight. I want us to make beautiful babies tonight. I'll play the guitar like the wind for you.

(Augie finally makes it to his feet. Nelly has an irresistible urge to help him. Augie lets go of the chair. Nelly gasps.)

NELLY: I prayed to God he'd get hit. I prayed he'd never walk again.

(Johnny grabs his guitar and tries to block Nelly's view of Augie.)

JOHNNY: I was in the garage. I sang. Something happened to my voice. It was amplified all over the San Fernando Valley and my voice bounced off the San Gabriel Mountains and young women heard it cruising down 101 and 405 and they drove red Fiats to my door.

(We see a projection of women listening to music.)

NELLY *(Not listening)*: My gray eye is killing me. *His* eye. I'm getting headaches and I can't sleep.

(Augie reaches for his zipper. But as he tries to unzip his pants, he loses his balance and falls. Nelly screams. Johnny pulls an orange from the tree.)

JOHNNY: Have an orange with me.

(Nelly ignores Johnny. She watches Augie lying helpless on the ground. Offstage, his wife laughs as garbage begins to fall on the prostrate Augie from above. Nelly tries to keep from sobbing.)

Scene Eight

A spotlight on the garage. Johnny is happily playing guitar for an invisible crowd of admirers.

JOHNNY: I know the business is hot now. You're going to open a new "Nelly and Johnny's" in Encino. But I've been thinking of other things. In a city that worships beauty like mine . . . where men without half my looks drive Porsches *that I have to fix* . . . I'm no longer content putting my eight-by-ten glossies in people's glove compartments. That will never make me a famous model.

(Spotlight on Nelly, in center room, looking at Augie.)

NELLY: There are women driving into the garage every day. They come to look at you and they drive red Fiats. Isn't that enough?
JOHNNY: That's only a handful of women. Not even ten.
NELLY: What do you want? *Millions* of women to want you?
JOHNNY: Well . . . yeah . . . why not? *(He laughs)* The other day, a woman in a red Fiat pulls in. She runs the biggest modeling agency in the southland. She has wild red hair and beautiful gorgeous white striking perfect little hands. She's in my fan club. *(He laughs again)* I happen to have my shirt off. She's staring at the thin sweaty finger of black hair that starts at my navel and points down, who-knows-where. She called me provocative. She gave me her card. In deference to you, I ripped it up. But then I taped it back together. But I ripped it up again. But I taped it back together. But I ripped it up again . . .

Scene Nine

Nelly goes to Augie. Augie is under a pile of old food, pizza boxes, newspapers, candy wrappers, beer cans, dirty Pampers, etc. The smell in the room makes Nelly want to gag.

Johnny angrily turns to face Nelly. From underneath the garbage, Augie groans.

AUGIE *(In pain)*: OooooOooooOooooOooooOoooo . . .
JOHNNY: The three of us will kill each other.
NELLY: I can make it work.
AUGIE: OooooooooOoooooOoooooooooo . . . !
NELLY: I've eaten those oranges. I'm bigger and smarter. I see him for what he is—
JOHNNY: A hardened, indecent, cockroach version of a man.
NELLY: Dying.
AUGIE: I said: oooooOoooooooooooooooOooooo.
JOHNNY: His death will be a mercy for all of us.
NELLY: If I'm one person, I'm three. You, me, and—
JOHNNY: Bring him here and you'll be only two. You and—
NELLY: Don't threaten me, Johnny, I—
AUGIE: I repeat: oooOoooooooooooooooOooooo!

(Nelly approaches the pile of garbage warily. She uncovers Augie. He is motionless. There's mold growing on his arms, mushrooms growing out of his chair. Nelly angrily opens the bedroom door.)

NELLY: What the hell's wrong with you, Mom?! There's mold growing on your husband and all you can do is screw teenage boys! *(She slams the door and runs offstage)*
JOHNNY: Okay. I'll go to this party tonight. Behind your back. I'll go with the woman in the red Fiat and the white hands who says I'm provocative. I'll play my guitar like old times.

(A projection of Johnny wearing a tuxedo. It says: "Johnny Amengual, Model." He looks at himself and smiles.
Nelly enters with a sponge and water. She cleans the mold from Augie's arms then carries him back to the wheelchair.)

NELLY: The smell of animal shit in this house is nauseating. On the tenth floor you can hear the spider monkeys. They're big now. Eating Lizbeth's old toys. Playing with Sylvia's clothes. Wearing her shorts. Peeing on her bed. Warthogs are walking through Antonio's room. They're getting big ideas about turning you into lunch. *(Beat)* It's Nelly. Remember? Dad? No? Well, I'm taking you to Los Angeles. Eat this orange.

(Nelly gives Augie an orange. He eats viciously. Augie visibly improves, as if electricity were shooting through his body. He glares at Nelly.)

Hi.

AUGIE: Don't give me hi! There was a mold formation on my arms!

NELLY: Dad, I didn't have to come back—

AUGIE: —and do you know what your mother's doing in the next room? Huh, Pinhead?

NELLY: I am not a pinhead! And Mom was lonely! Your accident made her lonely.

AUGIE: That's heartbreaking! Of course, I wasn't lonely. I had the company of flies. The friendship of lice. She starves me! My children starve me. Why are my children doing this to me?

(Nelly walks away from Augie.)

NELLY: Because you were a piece of shit as a father, that's why.

AUGIE: What'd you say to me? I was a great father! I gave birth to twenty-one—

NELLY: Wrong, Dad. *Mom* gave birth. You gave *zip*. You weren't around. You were partying. *(Beat)* We taught ourselves language, Dad. *There were no adults to teach us words.* That's why Primitivo, Nilda, and Heriberto can't even *speak.* Did you know that? No! You just thought they were shy! Lizbeth and Felicia speak in rhyme. Ping speaks in commercials. Gloria speaks nonsense. *Walking?!* Did you ever teach your kids walking? Anita hops like a rabbit. Rosaline walks on her hands. Social graces? Morals? Justice? *Hygiene?* No one taught us. Your poor children are compulsive liars and pyromaniacs and so love-starved, they'll sleep with the first person that smiles at them. *(Beat)* I grew up in the middle of the storm, Dad, overlooked, uncounted, just one of twenty-one

baby chicks, with my neck twisted up and my mouth open—
waiting for you to bring down a single dead worm for all of
us to eat and it wasn't enough, it was never enough, *and you
want to know why everyone left*?!

(Beat.)

AUGIE: Go back to California if you're going to be rude!

(Nelly turns away from him in disgust.)

NELLY: Oh, Dad . . . *(She faces Johnny)*
AUGIE: And you know how your mother spent all the insurance
money from the accident? Bought those four new Cadillacs
sitting outside. And a new bed. A ten-thousand-dollar bed
made out of *rose quartz*. And now she and her boyfriend are
going on a vacation—that my shattered spine is paying for—
to the Galápagos Islands!

(Nelly wanders away from Augie.)

NELLY: What did I come here to do, Johnny? Who is this old man
and what do I want from him?

(Johnny continues staring at the projection.)

JOHNNY: I wish I could help you. But I'm looking at something
so beautiful . . .

*(Nelly turns to Augie, determined. She's made up her mind and
she's resolved to go all the way.)*

NELLY: C'mon, we're getting out of here.
AUGIE: Where? To a nursing home to rot—?

(Nelly sweeps all the garbage offstage.)

NELLY: We can afford you now. We have money. A VCR. A side-by-side refrigerator stuffed with mangoes and arugula.

AUGIE: I will not live with Johnny Amengual.

NELLY: I've been working hard. Doing things no one ever taught me. Me and my *brains*.

AUGIE: I'll die in your house. I'll expire in two weeks, tops.

NELLY: But now I need a secretary. That's where you come in. It's light typing and phone. You don't need your legs for that.

AUGIE: A week and a half, max.

NELLY: A job will give you a purpose, keep your mind active, and it's not charity. It's the start of a new life, like it or not.

(Nelly exits with Augie.)

JOHNNY *(To projection)*: I have to find you Johnny Amengual, Model. Because she's doing it. She's bringing the butcher into my house.

(Lights out on Johnny. The projection disappears. Nelly reenters, pushing Augie, who is now sitting in a state-of-the-art wheelchair.)

Scene Ten

Johnny works on the car engine. Nelly wheels Augie into the garage. He and Johnny never look at each other.

NELLY *(To Augie)*: I just took out a loan to finance the opening of a third "Nelly and Johnny's," off the Long Beach Freeway, Firestone Exit, Southgate. Johnny and I have quadrupled our net worth since the start of the fiscal year. But we're very exclusive. In the Calendar we were listed as one of the ten hippest places in L.A. to get your car fixed. Sean Penn brings his '65 Oldsmobile for tune-ups. We've jump-started Marlon Brando and realigned Jack Nicholson. *(She goes to Johnny and laughs)* They love Johnny. He's a brilliant mechanic.

(*Nelly puts her arms around Johnny and kisses him. They inter-twine rapidly. Augie watches, disgusted, as they walk offstage, kissing. Augie wheels himself out of the room. Lights change: it's night.*)

Scene Eleven

Augie is in the left area of the stage, lying on a hospital bed. His new room is a big improvement over the old one. There are plants, cozy pictures, etc. The rest of the house is completely black.

From offstage, we hear Nelly and Johnny making love. Augie listens, wide-eyed and revolted for a couple of moments. He covers his ears. He turns on his transistor radio. He hums. He tries any-thing he can to blot out the sound, but nothing works. He finally screams in frustration.

AUGIE: ARGHAAHAHHGRARGAHGAGGAHHAAAA!!

(*Beat. Nelly, quickly putting on a robe, enters.*)

NELLY (*Breathless*): What happened? Something happened?
AUGIE: Yes! I had a terrible dream!
NELLY: You scared me to death. I thought the Walk-In Killer was getting you . . .
AUGIE: An indecent dream and you were in it.
NELLY: . . . but you'll *live*, right? Go back to sleep . . .
AUGIE: Then I was seized by unbearable, wretching, cataclysmic pain in the soles of my feet.
NELLY: You have no feeling in your feet.
AUGIE: My heart! Shooting, blistering, electric pain in the soles of my heart!
JOHNNY (*Offstage*): Nelllyy! Come back!
NELLY: One second!
AUGIE: I can't deal with L.A. Too many highways. Too much sun. Palm trees are weird. And there are rats living here!
NELLY: They live in the ivy *outside*.

AUGIE: They carry the plague. And they haven't caught the Hillside Strangler yet. And now there's this new one running around dressed up funny and cutting off your head politely. The Ninja Slasher.

NELLY *(Yawns)*: No. That's the Sepulveda Slasher. You're thinking of the Ninja Rapist.

JOHNNY *(Offstage)*: Nelly, *please*! Give me a break!

AUGIE: And I hate my job! My ear hurts because of that stupid telephone. Jack Nicholson was snotty to me. I'm going on strike.

NELLY: Go on strike, Dad, I'll cut your wages.

AUGIE: How can I pay the rent if you cut my wages?

NELLY: Exactly.

AUGIE: This is not how you treat a loving parent who gave you every advantage—

NELLY: That's true too.

AUGIE: I will not live with your revenge. I'd rather die than give you revenge!

NELLY *(Tired)*: I'm not trying to get revenge. I'm just . . . trying . . . to help you *make* something of yourself—

AUGIE *(Softly)*: I want my legs back. I want God to give me back my old life. The fun. The girls. I'm dead down there. If I can't sleep with a woman, what good am I? *(Quickly)* Find me a goat. If I kill a goat and wash my legs in its blood, I'll be walking in two weeks—

JOHNNY *(Offstage)*: Hey Nellllllllllllllllyyyyyyyy! Come back to bed! I didn't finish yet! I have to finish!

NELLY: See you in the morning, Dad.

AUGIE: And please don't sleep with him anymore. I can't take it. He can finish his dirty business alone.

JOHNNY *(Offstage)*: NO I CAN'T! NELLLLLLLLLLYYYYYYYYYY!

NELLY *(To Augie)*: Get some sleep. I'll see you later.

(Nelly kisses Augie and quickly exits.)

JOHNNY *(Offstage)*: Thank God you're back! Are you ready?

(We hear Nelly and Johnny making love again. Beat.)

AUGIE: Ahhhhhghghh! No! Nooooooo! Don't cut my throat! Don't kill me, please!

(Nelly enters, putting on her robe. She gives Augie a murderous look. Augie smiles sheepishly. Lights start to fade. Augie's smile turns into a laugh that echoes hauntingly in the coming blackout.

Before the lights disappear, Nelly grabs her head as if getting a searing headache and we see a projection of Johnny wearing a white mask.

Blackout.)

ACT TWO

Scene One

A few months later. Lights up only on the orange tree. One by one, a third of the oranges in the tree turn black.

Scene Two

It's morning. Nelly, Augie and Johnny are in the center room having breakfast. Johnny is in coveralls. Nelly is in a nice business suit. Augie is in Star Wars *pajamas.*

No one eats. No one speaks. No one looks at the other person. Finally:

NELLY: I heard on the radio: there's a hurricane coming from Japan. Be here today. Big mother hurricane the size of a hundred dragons. *(She laughs)* Maybe it'll drop Toshiba microwaves on us! Huh? Nissan trucks and baby Godzillas falling from the sky! Paper birds. Sushi rain.

(No one laughs.)

I made plans for this hurricane. You both have specific duties for this emergency plan of mine.

(No one says anything for a while.)

AUGIE: I have a complaint to make.
JOHNNY: Don't say a word. Not. A. Single. Friggin'. Word.

(Silence.)

AUGIE: The hash browns? They suck.
JOHNNY: I said don't complain!

(Longer silence.)

AUGIE: Hash browns should be crispy.
JOHNNY: Hash browns are any damn way I make 'em, pal. I am an excellent cook. I am multifaceted.

(Silence.)

AUGIE: My room is too small. I want a bigger room. I want northern exposure.

(Nelly quickly takes out a small notebook and reads from it.)

NELLY: First, I'll shut down the garage. Disconnect the gas. Tape up windows. These are your duties, gentlemen. Dad, number one—
JOHNNY *(To Nelly)*: You ruined our paradise. Brought the friggin' serpent from Hell into our living room. So shut up.
AUGIE: Don't talk to my daughter that way.
JOHNNY: Your daughter? Your daughter? Your daughter? Your daughter? Your *daughter*? Don't tell me about your daughter—
AUGIE: I bet you can tell me all sorts of things about my daughters! Like which ones gave birth to your bastards before their sixteenth birthdays—

JOHNNY: *At least I loved them . . .*
AUGIE: How many of my babies' hearts did you break—?
JOHNNY: At least I know this one's name!
AUGIE: I do too! I do too! Her name is Carol!
JOHNNY: Her name is not Carol!
AUGIE: Claudette?

(Johnny grabs his guitar and starts to leave.)

NELLY: Where are you going?
JOHNNY: There's always a party in Los Angeles. Look for me there.
AUGIE: Krista!
NELLY: We have to work on this. There's a hurricane—
AUGIE: Karen—
NELLY: *Nelly*—
AUGIE: I said my room sucks! I wouldn't keep a dog in that room. And why haven't you blessed me with legitimate grandchildren yet? What kind of man are you, anyway?

(Johnny lunges at Augie. Loud hurricane winds. Thunder and lightning. We see a projection of a palm tree bent over by the wind.)

JOHNNY: Goddamn *everything.*

(Johnny goes to the garage. He closes windows, locks doors, etc. Nelly wheels Augie to his bed as the lightning quickens.)

AUGIE: He's screwing other women. I can see it. I can tell.
NELLY: Keep your filthy mouth off him.
AUGIE: His walk is funny. He walks like a man screwing somebody who's not his wife.

(Nelly angrily starts preparing Augie's bed.)

JOHNNY: Gloria. Come rescue me! I'm in prison with your gelatinous old man and his gray gummy runny mucky fault-finding eyes.

(The wind picks up. There's a projection of Gloria. Johnny sees the projection and kisses it as the wind howls.)

NELLY *(To Augie)*: You? Bed.

(Nelly starts to lift Augie into bed. Johnny kisses the projection of Gloria. He starts taking off his shirt. Lightning. Thunder. Gloria's projection turns off, along with all the lights onstage. It's a total blackout.
Johnny grabs flashlights and goes to Augie and Nelly. He gives Nelly and Augie a flashlight each. Augie is still in his chair, his radio playing. The storm gets louder, crazier. Johnny looks out the window.)

JOHNNY: There are palm trees flying around! Cars going up in the air! All the stars on Hollywood Boulevard are whirling around like comets! The Hollywood Hills are cracking open and foul brown human cesspool goo is pouring out! If we only had a radio!

NELLY: Dad's got a radio.

JOHNNY: Augie's got a radio?

AUGIE: Don't get any ideas about this radio, junior. I'm listening to comedy.

JOHNNY: I want to hear the weather on the radio!

AUGIE *(Listening to radio)*: "The batter hits it to the shortstop. The shortstop throws it to the first baseman. Who gets it? Exactly."

JOHNNY: Listen to that wind! That's a wind we've never heard before. No one knows what's coming.

(Johnny yanks the radio out of Augie's hands. He throws the radio on the ground, smashing it. Augie looks at him in disbelief.)

AUGIE: I'll kill you. No. I'll mutilate you first, then I'll kill you.

(Augie wheels himself to the bed. Lights up full all over the stage: power has returned. From under his pillow, Augie pulls out a massive machete. He goes after Johnny full speed. Johnny laughs.)

Don't laugh at me!

(Nelly lies on the hospital bed, playing with the buttons, making the bed go up and down. Johnny dances around Augie, taunting him. Augie nearly hits him several times.)

JOHNNY: You're a joke! You're a vast human joke!
AUGIE: And you're going to be little, tiny, compact pieces of dead mechanic! Little, tiny, bloody, painful pieces of dead shit!

(As Augie continues to swing the machete, Johnny plays his guitar, dancing around Augie. Augie stops, exhausted. Nelly continues playing with the bed.)

My daughter isn't the only one with funny gray eyes. Look at mine. They're gray too. I can see the future too. You're going to die twice, Johnny Amengual. All men die once. But you're going to die twice.

(As Johnny continues to dance and play the guitar, lights start to fade. In the dark, it's Johnny's wild laugh that echoes. Blackout.)

Scene Three

Lights up on garage. Johnny is working on the car engine. Augie, in his chair stage left, is flipping over tarot cards. Nelly is on the sofa in the center room, vainly trying to concentrate on bookkeeping.

As Augie flips cards, Johnny holds his head as if going through an intense headache.

AUGIE: Johnny is vain. Johnny is ignorant. Johnny is perverted. Johnny is empty-headed. Johnny is lazy. Johnny is rude. Johnny is redundant. Johnny is derivative. Johnny is indecent. *(He smiles)* Gloria!

(Johnny hears "Gloria." He looks around, trying to figure out where the word came from.)

JOHNNY: Gloria.

(We see a projection of Gloria. Johnny can't help but look at her. Augie chants:)

AUGIE: Gloria is beautiful. Gloria is amoral. Gloria is self-actual-ized. Gloria is user-friendly. Gloria is upwardly mobile. Gloria is tax-exempt. Gloria is a virgin.

JOHNNY AND AUGIE: Gloria is a whore. Gloria is growth oriented. Gloria is bicoastal. Gloria is generous. Gloria is waiflike. Gloria is legal.

AUGIE: Johnny! I'm legal!

(Johnny looks around. He rubs his throbbing head.)

JOHNNY: Gloria?
AUGIE: It's my birthday.
JOHNNY: Wait, wait a min—
AUGIE: I'm legal.
JOHNNY: . . . this is crazy; where . . . are . . . you . . . ?
AUGIE: It's my birthday.
JOHNNY: It's a headache.
AUGIE: I'm legal.
JOHNNY: . . . aspirin, Johnny . . . you need to get some asp—
AUGIE: It's my birthday.
JOHNNY: Gloria? *Where? Are? You?*
AUGIE: I'm legal.
JOHNNY: Really?
AUGIE: It's my birthday.
JOHNNY: I . . . I . . . don't believe . . .
AUGIE: I'm legal.
JOHNNY: I miss you. Is this real—?
AUGIE: It's my birthday.
JOHNNY: I know, baby! I know!
AUGIE: I'm legal.

JOHNNY: That's great. But.

AUGIE: It's my birthday.

JOHNNY: But. No. I love Nell—

AUGIE: I'm legal.

JOHNNY: I need . . . to get out of here . . . I need . . .

AUGIE: It's my birthday.

JOHNNY: . . . to play the guitar . . . have a little fun . . .

AUGIE: I'm legal.

JOHNNY: . . . Gloria?

AUGIE: Go.

JOHNNY: I need to go.

AUGIE: Go.

JOHNNY: Being a mechanic sucks . . .

AUGIE: *Go!*

(*Gloria's projection disappears. Johnny hurriedly takes off his coveralls—he's got party clothes underneath. He combs his hair, grabs his guitar. He and Nelly look at each other.*
During the following scene, Augie looks at his tarot cards as if they were Nelly and Johnny.)

JOHNNY: I can't anymore, Nelly, I can't!

AUGIE: It's my birthday!

JOHNNY: I don't know what's wrong—it could be an earthquake I feel vibrating in my bones like a bad omen—

NELLY: You're working too hard, John—

JOHNNY: I'm full of *static* . . . white noise behind my damn *eyes* . . .

NELLY: Come here. Sit with me.

JOHNNY: No! It's not fatigue. It's the day. It's Gloria's birthday, Nel. She's legal today.

AUGIE: I'm legal!

JOHNNY: She's been shoved into my mind, Nelly. She's telling me to break open the night and be wild in it.

AUGIE: It's my birthday!

JOHNNY: I looked at my greasy clothes today. The smell of transmission fluid and dirty valves. I'm permeated with this job, Nelly. It came to me today: I don't love my talent for cars.

AUGIE: I'm legal.

JOHNNY: I have to quit "Nelly and Johnny's." I'm ready to go. To start my true career as a model because I will never be better looking than I am now!

NELLY: Because it's Gloria's birthday?

JOHNNY: Because it's time. And we have security. A bank full of money. Forty-six skilled mechanics who can cover for me—

NELLY: Because it's Gloria's birthday?

JOHNNY: Because it's *me*. This is the man you married. I tried to do it your way . . . I worked hard . . . and I'm dead tired because my heart was never in it and I suffered too much.

(Johnny goes to Nelly. She holds him. Augie holds the tarot cards in the air.)

AUGIE: Let him go let him go let him go let him go . . .

NELLY *(To Johnny)*: Go do what you want. Please go do what you want. Just—don't turn me into a jailer. I'm not your goddamn jailer.

(Johnny looks at her, shocked—then jumps.)

JOHNNY: All right! Oh this is it! Look out America! I'm going to be mobbed when I step out of the house in the morning! I'm going to be incredibly snotty to many people!

(Nelly laughs. Johnny looks at her.)

You don't mind? Do you mind? You mind, right?

NELLY: We were a great team, Johnny.

JOHNNY: Why don't you quit too? It can't be fun for you anymore. It's a machine. *Dump* it.

NELLY: But I love this machine.

JOHNNY: Then just go out with me tonight. Put on your best dress. Every jewel you own. Something sparkly and diamond-like that'll shiver when you dance.

NELLY: I can't.

JOHNNY: Come on! One little night! This is a party town! We'll dress up like barbarians and drive Martin Sheen's Porsche.

NELLY: I just can't. I'm too afraid.

JOHNNY: Of having a little fun?

NELLY: Of turning my back on the work I have to do.

JOHNNY: For one night?

NELLY: I don't want everything to disappear when I'm not looking. Things have been disappearing from my life for as long as I remember.

JOHNNY: That was your old life.

NELLY: Clothes, people, food—*food already in my stomach* has been taken away from me. If I stop working . . . if I let down for just one night . . . I'll start speaking in nonsense . . . walking around on all fours . . .

JOHNNY: I know what's happening. It's. It's *him*. Augie.

AUGIE: Don't blame me! Hey!

JOHNNY: He's doing something to you too. He's bringing that old life back to you.

NELLY: You can't blame him for everything. I laid down the law with him. He's quiet. Hardly leaves his room now.

JOHNNY: He's doing something. Putting things in the food.

NELLY: He stopped doing that a long time ago—

JOHNNY *(Desperate)*: *Something's* changed with me. I don't dream in color anymore. When I *think* . . . I can't hear my voice too well . . . I miss the sound of my *thoughts*, Nelly . . . he's taken that away.

AUGIE: I can't do that! I never learned to do that!

NELLY: Johnny, all he's doing is his goat ritual. He wants to kill a goat, wash his legs in its blood, and walk again.

JOHNNY: Let him. Let him walk three thousand miles out of our lives.

NELLY: No sacrificial killing in my house!

JOHNNY: But all the oranges are turning *black* because of him! He's back in your blood. He controls your sleep. He controls your dreams. He's *corrupting* you. And did you notice? Now our house is getting bigger! There are rooms up there starting to grow!

NELLY: That's crazy—

JOHNNY: Well, he's not going to corrupt me! I'm going out to find some fun! I'm going to find my fan club! To find the lady in the red Fiat! *(He grabs his guitar and starts to exit. He looks at Nelly)* I miss the old times, Nelly. When guys would bristle when I walked into a room and all their women looked at me. When I made time stop. People would whisper about me. Hearts would beat fast. Men would reach for their guns. Who would I talk to? Who would I dance with? Who would I touch? I have to prove I have the old magic.

NELLY: Be careful. You'll get yourself killed, Johnny.

(Johnny leaves. Augie clasps his hands in prayer and looks up at the sky.)

AUGIE: I owe you one, Big Guy.

Scene Four

Exhausted, Nelly lies on the sofa in the center room. Her eyes hurt. As Augie wheels himself around and around her, time passes rapidly. Black and white clouds pass overhead. Nelly tries to sleep and can't.

AUGIE: He was right. I am part of you again. I'm your angel. I'm back in your blood.

NELLY: What are you doing to him? I keep hearing the flap-flap-flap of tarot cards in your room.

AUGIE: He knows it's Gloria's birthday because *those two are linked.* They're going to be together no matter what you do, Carmen.

NELLY: My name's not Carmen!

AUGIE: You have to run. Tonight. Run with me to the old house and live like old times.

NELLY: I will never go back there.

AUGIE: You're smart and strong and beautiful. There's no reason to live your life for him *when you can live your life for me.* I'll always appreciate you, Cathy.

NELLY *(Tired)*: That's not my name!

AUGIE: Doesn't matter what your name is. You're *my* girl. Augie's girl. The one I *knew* would come back and clean the sticky mold off my body—

NELLY: I'm tired, Dad. I'm really tired. And I don't trust you.

AUGIE: You married him to get out of my house. But there's no escaping my house. It's always with you. Always growing in you, room after unbelievable room, containing strange and magical things.

NELLY *(More to herself)*: My eyes hurt. If I don't go to sleep now, I'll be awake the rest of the month . . .

AUGIE: Don't fight me.

NELLY: . . . and I don't want to start seeing the future. I don't want to start seeing things I don't want to see!

AUGIE: You think you can remake the world. Turn Johnny into an honest man. Make us all live together. Well you can't. You're not that strong.

NELLY: And you. No *more*—please—find yourself a friggin' goat—kill it—walk again—and get the hell out of my house! You're fired! I'm getting someone else to work for me. I'm sending you back to Mom.

AUGIE: You're confused.

NELLY: Don't tell me that!

(She slaps Augie. Johnny staggers into the center room, guitar shattered, clothes torn and face bloody. He stands in a special light. Augie wheels himself to his bedroom. Nelly looks at her husband in shock.)

JOHNNY: It was six of them against me . . . six jealous husbands . . . at least seven feet tall . . .

NELLY: I'll kill them. Whoever touched you, I'll get them, Johnny.

JOHNNY: . . . I fought back . . . I hit them hard . . . but their bodies were made of rock and they broke my hands . . .

NELLY: What did they look like? Where did they go?

JOHNNY: . . . the husbands were pissed . . . didn't like my fan club . . . six animals in black tie and brass knuckles and steel-pointed boots and not a teardrop's worth of mercy . . .

(Nelly cleans Johnny's bloody face. Augie stifles a laugh and starts flipping over tarot cards. Nelly takes Johnny to the sofa and he lies down.)

Scene Five

Lights change. Nelly is on the phone, Johnny on the sofa, Augie is in his area stage left.

NELLY: I want police protection. For my husband. He's been getting death threats. Jealous husbands have burned him in effigy on La Cienega Boulevard. Armies of angry men come here daily to shake dangerous weapons in his face. I want a cop in front of the garage twenty-four hours a day. And a police escort to follow Johnny to all the modeling agencies in town. As soon as his face clears, he's going to have a big career as a model. Yes, Johnny is too beautiful to live! Yes, it's the kind of beauty other men want to kill him for. Do I have to get a gun? I have chic friends with guns. I'll protect him myself!

(Nelly hangs up. Augie goes to Johnny, whispers.)

AUGIE: You're going back out.

(Johnny sits up, dazed, rubbing his head.)

JOHNNY: I'm going back out.
NELLY: You're not going anywhere.
JOHNNY: There's a party somewhere in Los Angeles.
NELLY: You're delirious.
JOHNNY: I'm going back out.
AUGIE: Let him go out! A man shouldn't be afraid to leave his house.
JOHNNY: I'm not afraid. I'm going out. There's a party somewhere in Los Angeles!
NELLY: You're not going anywhere.

AUGIE *(To Johnny)*: Are you afraid? Or are you a man?

JOHNNY: I'm a man! I'm a man! I'm a man!

(Johnny starts to wobble to the door. Nelly exits and reenters with a revolver. She points it at Johnny.)

NELLY: I happen to be real serious about this. I want obedience in this matter! I know about danger. I was raised on it. It was in the milk. It sets off a vibration in your gut, in the frightened liquids of your intestines: my dreams are thick with it. I'm closing the garage. Sealing us off from the rest of the world until I figure out what to do about this danger.

(Johnny lies on the sofa. Nelly goes to the garage. As she enters, she sees something on the ground and screams, Johnny sits up startled, and a projection of a human hand is shown.)

JOHNNY *(Stunned)*: Did he have to do that to her? Did he have to chop off her hand? It was innocent! She wanted to know where I got my hair cut. What diet I was on. What gym I worked out at.

(Nelly rushes to Johnny, shaking, frightened.)

Now her jealous husband's chopped off the beautiful hand that never touched me but wanted to . . .

NELLY: Oh Johnny. My eyes have been totaled by that amputated hand on the garage floor—oh—God—how that poor woman must have suffered . . .

JOHNNY: My face. My beautiful face. I did that to her.

(Nelly is fighting her body's tendency to drop down on all fours.)

NELLY: No. No. *Upright* Nelly. Be upright. Don't sink back, that's what your enemies want.

JOHNNY: How many more will suffer for me?

(The projection of the severed hand disappears.)

NELLY: This wasn't just an act of cruelty. It signals war. They're coming for you. *(She exits and reenters with a bulletproof vest)* They're capable of anything. Even if we lock the doors and smother ourselves behind barred windows, they'll find a way in. Armed Response won't stop them. *(She puts on the vest)* I know where they live. I have lists. I know all the red Fiats we repaired. I know where they get together to plot severed hands and mayhem. *(She sticks the revolver into her belt. She goes to Augie. She searches his room for the machete)*

AUGIE: You won't find them.

NELLY: I have lists! Computer lists. Shut up. You think I'm weak? You think I'm still that four-legged little mouse you used to bat around? I'm about to fulfill my potential.

AUGIE: Ain't feminine.

NELLY: Is too! Where's the fucking machete? *(She finds the machete)* Ah-ha! You're going to stand guard. Okay? Just do it. I won't be home. I have a mission.

AUGIE: All your energy wasted being tough.

NELLY: It's how I survived your house, Dad. Now. I don't want you to let anyone in. If they come near my husband, I want you to slash them thoroughly. *(She hands him the machete)* If I come home and he's dead . . . I will take this machete and amputate your lifeless dick.

(Nelly kisses Augie on the cheek, goes to Johnny and kisses him.)

NELLY: And you. Step out of the house, I'll kill you. Bye, honey.

(Nelly exits. With the machete on his lap, Augie wheels himself to Johnny in the center room. He watches Johnny sleep. He lifts the machete in the air as if about to chop Johnny's head off.)

AUGIE: Hey! Are you my goat?! Are you the sacrifice I need?

JOHNNY *(Asleep)*: Gotta get new pictures.

AUGIE: You're as good as a goat. Stupid like a goat. I could cut your friggin' head right off. Smear your blood all over my legs, wash them real good, and run away and be happy the rest of my life.

JOHNNY *(Asleep)*: Get some new clothes. Drop ten pounds. Now that Nelly's behind me, I'm going far.

(Augie lifts the machete as if to cut off Johnny's head. He brings down the machete swiftly—but stops himself at the last second. He brings the sharp edge of the machete gently down on Johnny's neck and laughs.)

AUGIE: There are better ways, Augie. Less blood.

(The projection of Gloria is seen.)

Johnny!

JOHNNY: Gloria!

AUGIE: It's me, baby. Tell me. Are all those messy death threats and severed hands getting you down?

JOHNNY: I'm scared.

AUGIE: Don't be blue, Johnny. There's good news. I'm in town. I'm here in Los Angeles.

JOHNNY: You are?

AUGIE: And guess what! I have two-color eyes. I talk to my big sisters. Lizbeth, Maritza, and Felicia tell me how wonderful you are.

JOHNNY: Come over here!

AUGIE: I can't. Your wife what's-her-name is there. Come to me. I'm at the Toluca Lake Capri Motel.

JOHNNY: I can't leave. Nelly'd kill me.

AUGIE: Once we're together, I can give you the life you want.

JOHNNY: Jealous men will firebomb me if they see me in my car.

(The projection of a car is seen.)

AUGIE: I know you can't be satisfied by one woman. You need new women with new eyes. Soon, my little sister Anita will be legal in many states. When that day comes, I'll cheerfully let you go . . .

JOHNNY: You will? *(Quickly)* But they'll burn me.

AUGIE: I'm here one night. This is our last chance.

JOHNNY: . . . I want to . . .

AUGIE: So get in your car, pick two fat oranges from your magic tree and meet me at the Toluca Lake Capri Motel.

(Johnny goes to the orange tree and picks two huge oranges.)

JOHNNY: Nelly . . . ?

AUGIE: My father will cover for you. He'll swear you were here all night.

(Johnny looks around.)

JOHNNY: Nell? I'm sorry. She's in my blood. I'm a weak man. I'm not good like you.

(Johnny exits. Hold on projection of the car. Augie pops a wheelie and holds up the machete, victorious.)

Scene Six

As Augie laughs, Nelly enters the center room, her gun smoking. She seems intoxicated.

NELLY: Johnny! Johnny! Haha! I was your Clint Eastwood, Johnny! And they made my day!

AUGIE: He's not here. He's out fooling around. Cheating on you.

NELLY *(Laughing)*: I didn't kill. But I maimed. I left behind a few legs with holes in them, a few splintered bones, and some shot-up hands. I blasted their cars to rusty pulp!

AUGIE: Doing it with your baby sister in a cheap Toluca Lake motel. I begged him not to go out.

NELLY: We live in a safe world. I cleaned it out for you. It's now safe for people who love each other like you and me.

(A huge explosion! The projection of the car is replaced by a projection of a car in flames.

Johnny staggers in, clothes smoking. He covers his face with his hands. Nelly attends to him as if putting out a fire on his body. The projection of the flaming car disappears.

Lights down low until there's only light around Nelly and Johnny.)

Scene Seven

Tableau: Nelly holding Johnny. Johnny facing upstage. Nelly facing downstage. Augie in darkness.

JOHNNY: Nelly, they rigged the car.

NELLY: You'll be out of the hospital in one month. *(Beat)* We lost the garage. It went up in flames. People are avoiding "Nelly and Johnny's." The Calendar's listed us as one of the top ten places to avoid in Los Angeles. *(Beat)* Your body wasn't touched by the fire—but you didn't escape the flames altogether.

JOHNNY: When can I go home? I feel fine. I don't have a single burn.

NELLY: Remember that it doesn't matter. Nothing's changed. You're still the same man. I still love you. *(She holds up a white mask)*

JOHNNY: Why did they cover all the mirrors in my room?

NELLY: The jealous men have stolen your precious beauty from this unlucky world. It's your first death—my father predicted it.

JOHNNY: I'm all right! I'm fine! I wasn't touched!

NELLY: So this is your new face.

JOHNNY: Why do they keep me here? *(He turns to face the audience)*

NELLY: Look up. Up.

JOHNNY: Why did they cover all the mirrors in my room?

(Johnny looks up. Nelly brings the mask down on his face. When it touches him, he screams. Nelly straps the skintight mask to his face and holds him.)

Scene Eight

Nelly takes Johnny to the sofa. Augie is joyfully flipping over tarot cards, barely able to contain his glee. Augie wears a Walkman.

NELLY: Dinner—will be—will be—ready—*okay, I will not start talking funny! (Slow)* I can't—be—slipping—back. You see what happens Johnny? Everything goes! I will straighten up my speech! Grief will not destroy my language! *(Determined)* Dinner will be ready in a couple of minutes! *(Beat, normal)* Dinner will be ready in a couple of minutes. *(Beat)* It hurts to walk upright. Your accident's made my back curve down. Ever since your fire. Ever since your meltdown. But I'm holding myself up. For you and Dad and what's left of the business—I'm engaged in a struggle to *make life work again.* There will be fresh asparagus for dinner. Mashed potatoes, roast beef and fresh milk. Okay?

(Nelly waits. No response from Johnny.)

AUGIE: He always traded on his good looks to get away with murder. What's he going to do without his secret weapon?
NELLY: He's going to survive on my strength.
AUGIE: Yours? Are you stupid? Did you see the get-well cards from all the women he used to sing for?
NELLY: I beat my past. I slaughtered my inheritance. I maimed my bad speech and my crooked legs. I will beat this catastrophe too, Dad.
AUGIE: You know he keeps that woman's severed hand in a baggie? Look in your closet. It's there. Next to the shoes. He can look at it every day and remember the power of his lost beauty.
NELLY: Get up and let's have dinner, Johnny.

(She waits. He's motionless.)

No? You're not hungry? *(Beat. Soft)* Maybe you'll eat an orange with me? Oranges always make you want to play guitar.

(Nelly kisses Johnny and takes his hand.)

The modeling agencies have been calling nonstop. They loved your old pictures. They can find you work instantly. Uhm. I told them you weren't available. They offered big contracts and I had to say no. I burned all your old pictures, Johnny, I had to. *(Beat)* I don't care about it. Means nothing to me. Your face was not what I loved when I loved.

(Nelly, trying not to cry, exits. Lights fall. It's night.)

Scene Nine

Johnny on the sofa. Augie in the center room. Nelly enters center room with a box of masks.

NELLY: Look at me. I understand it's hard, Johnny. I'm suffering too. But I have to *do* something. I have to keep *moving.* *(Beat)* I reopened "Nelly and Johnny's." I'm working again. Twenty-four hours a day. Got on the phone to old customers. Begged them to come back. Told them it's safe. They're coming back!

(No response. Nelly looks at him a while.)

Try these other masks. Maybe you'll feel better.

(Nelly takes a mask out of the box. It's a Cary Grant mask. She puts it over Johnny's white mask. She doesn't like the way it looks. She tries another mask—a Donald Duck mask. That doesn't look right either and she tries another.)

(To Augie:) I told his little groupies to go to hell. I threatened to blow them away.

AUGIE: Don't you ever give up? That's not a man. That's a tackling dummy.

NELLY: Did you see the *L.A. Times*? The jealous husbands have taken out a full-page ad congratulating themselves for doing this to Johnny. I should have killed them all.

AUGIE: Me? I'm a real man with real needs, but you ignore me for *that*.

NELLY: I'm going to make Johnny come back. I'm going to improve his self-image. Get him going again.

AUGIE: Listen. You have to do the only honorable thing. The only moral thing. A mercy killing.

NELLY *(Looks at him)*: What did you say?

AUGIE: He's worthless. At least I can answer the phone and type.

NELLY: He still has his hands! He can still function!

(Nelly pulls Johnny to the car engine. Augie follows.)

AUGIE: Just kill him! Kill him and remarry! Live in the old house with me! Fill the old house with twenty-one children!

(Nelly makes Johnny stand in front of the engine.)

NELLY: His hands have memories of usefulness and hard work. That's not dead in him.

AUGIE: You've got guns. It would be so easy to off him. And then you could blame it on a jealous husband—

NELLY: Johnny. This is Chevy engine. It needs a tune-up. Show me you can still do it. Show me you can still make it go.

(Johnny does not move.)

C'mon. You can do tune-ups in your sleep. Your hands are not burned. Your mind is not burned. Work is good for you. Work is important. Work keeps the spirit alive. Come on, Johnny.

(Johnny doesn't move. Nelly grabs his hands angrily.)

Are you in prison, Johnny? Well, I'm in prison too! God-damn you!

(Nelly lets his hands go and walks away.)

I put my hands on your face. After the fire. I was holding in the guts of your face. But you're lost. And now it looks like I'm lost too. *My* face is burned. My eyes are burned *white* . . . *(Fighting for control)* . . . white, my love, like the screaming brains trying to squeeze out of your eyes—blind old brains enraged with heat, trying to escape that hot oven and the simmering nerves and the baked memories and the bubbling dreams—just trying to run out of that head and into the cool air . . .

(Nelly turns away, not wanting to let Johnny see her cry. Augie looks at Nelly and smiles.)

AUGIE: Mercy. Killing. Today.

(Nelly moves to slap him across the face. He grabs her hand and stops her.)

Tonight, if you can sleep, dream the future, dream next year, and you'll see it doesn't contain him.

NELLY: I'm throwing you out!

AUGIE: I'm your father. I know what's best. I even know your name begins with an "N." I know more than he does!

NELLY: You're going back to Mom. GOING BACK TODAY!

AUGIE: That vegetable doesn't know anything. Ask him. Ask him your name!

NELLY: I don't have to test him.

AUGIE: What's your wife's name, Johnny?

NELLY: Leave him alone.

AUGIE: What is her name? Tell me her name!

NELLY *(To Johnny)*: Don't have to tell him anything!

(Beat.)

JOHNNY: I don't know.

(Beat.)

NELLY: What, Johnny?
AUGIE: He doesn't know.

(Beat.)

JOHNNY: I don't remember.
NELLY *(Shocked)*: It's Nelly. My—my—my—name—
JOHNNY: I don't know it. I'm sorry.
NELLY: Say name! My name! *(Panicking)* What's my goddamn name?

(Beat.)

JOHNNY: Pinhead . . . ?

(Augie laughs.)

NELLY: What?
AUGIE *(Laughing)*: Pinhead!
NELLY: Johnny?
AUGIE: He called you Pinhead!

(Augie laughs. Nelly leaves the stage. Augie sees his chance and hurries to Johnny.)

AUGIE: You smashed my radio. But I adapted. Now I have a Walkman. I'm a survivor. I don't think you're a survivor. You still smell like the fire. I lost my appetite for a week because of the barbecue smell of your skin. Wanna listen to my radio now?

(He puts the Walkman on Johnny. We hear horrible, dissonant sounds: human cries, wind, electric noise.)

Listen to the hurricane now. To the world out of control all around you. The chaos of deferred dreams. The riot of sexual rejection. You think Gloria wants to nuzzle up against that charred stump of yours? Or Anita? Or Rosaline?

(Augie takes the Walkman off Johnny. The sounds disappear.)

Your wife won't do you the favor of a mercy killing. So you have to take the initiative. A nice, clean suicide is the best way. *(He wheels himself to the orange tree)* See this? Some oranges have turned black. They're sour inside. They're no longer the sweet aphrodisiac you seduced my dear daughter what's-her-name with. The grief in this house has turned the juice in each orange into high-octane gasoline. Really flammable. Smell.

(Augie plucks a black orange from the tree and puts it under Johnny's nose. Johnny sniffs and quickly jerks away.)

Pure gasoline. Very explosive. The key to your freedom.

(Nelly enters with a suitcase. She goes to Augie.)

NELLY: I want you to get the hell out of my house!
AUGIE: Why? What'd I do . . . ?
NELLY: Get out, you parasitic, caustic, irrational, lethal, inconsiderate, possessive, demeaning, disgusting, degenerate old man!
AUGIE: Your name begins with an N! It's Naomi!
NELLY: *He* is the man I love! *He* went through hell for me. *He* gave up his dreams for me. I will not abandon such a man!
AUGIE: Norma? Nina?
NELLY: How could I have been so stupid? How could I not have seen you sooner? Seen you for what you really—really—really—really— *(She falls to the ground. She starts running around on all fours)*
AUGIE: That's my girl! That's the girl I love! I'll take care of you now!
NELLY: No—!
AUGIE: Run, run, little girl! You're so cute when you scamper!
NELLY: I can fight this—!
AUGIE: Your name! *It's coming back to me . . .*
NELLY: *. . . I can stop this . . .*

AUGIE: Ne—Ne—Ne—*Nel*—

NELLY: I'm fighting. I'm fighting. I'm fighting. *(She stops running)* I'm fighting you. *(She straightens up with great difficulty)*

AUGIE *(Panicking)*: Ne—Ne—*Nel*—Ne—Ne—

NELLY: Nelly, Nelly, it's Nelly— *(She dashes to Augie's suitcase)* You're going back home to Mom. Your bags are packed. You leave in one hour.

AUGIE: Let me prove I love you!

NELLY: I called home. Mom and her boyfriend are getting married and moving to the Galápagos Islands. You have the house all to yourself—

AUGIE: Johnny! Tell her I can't go back! I'll die in that house!

NELLY: I'll hire a nurse to walk you and cook for you.

AUGIE: Alone? With all the memories in that house?

NELLY: When Johnny's back on his feet, I'll visit you. Christmas maybe.

AUGIE: The animals! My grandchildren's hungry animals! They'll eat me alive!

NELLY: I hope so.

AUGIE: You're sending me to my death! I won't go!

(Nelly pulls out the revolver and points it at Augie.)

NELLY: You'll go. And you'll like it.

(Nelly picks up the suitcases and leaves the house. As Augie wheels himself out, he stops near Johnny.)

AUGIE: Remember to cleanse yourself, Johnny. In oranges. *(He wheels himself out)*

Scene Ten

Lights up in Augie's old bedroom left. Nelly is there. Augie sits in the square-wheeled chair.

NELLY: I can't believe how big the house has gotten. Almost covers the block.

AUGIE: I'll die of loneliness.

NELLY: You gave birth to twenty-one children, how can you be lonely?

AUGIE: I miss Los Angeles! The palm trees. The sun. The big lovely room I lived in. The Midnight Stalker! The plague!

(Nelly can barely look at him.)

NELLY: I don't know what to say to you, Dad. I thought there was something else in you. Something . . . what? . . . good? Does that word remotely apply to you? What was good, Dad? That you loved me enough to wish Johnny dead? Should that make me happy? *(Beat)* My gray eye. Gives me sight. That's from you. Sight is good. But when I think of some of the things you've said and done . . . I almost want to scrape my gray eye out with a stick, Dad, and go blind . . . *(She kisses him quickly. She starts to exit)*

AUGIE: Your name is Nelly.

(She stops. Augie can barely look at her.)

Nelly was your mother's mother's name. She was a brave old lady with different-color eyes who could see the future in her sleep. Old Nelly averted disasters by dreaming them before they happened. Hurricanes, droughts, insect invasions. But her talent took its toll. Every time she predicted a disaster she absorbed the fear for all her people and that made her gray, feeble, fragile, before her time. She drank heavily to calm her electrified nerves. She died young. A hero. Nelly is my eleventh child, my fifth daughter. Oscar, Maritza, Nilda, Heriberto, Carlos, Marcos, Beto, Lizbeth, Jesus, Felicia, Che, Gloria, Antonio, Anita, Rosaline, Primitivo, Ping, Sylvia, Linda, Freddie and the one who stuck by me the longest, the one we called Nelly.

(Nelly looks at her father. Lights up on the center room. Johnny sits motionless on the sofa, waiting.)

NELLY: Christmas. Maybe.

(Nelly exits. Augie is alone. Light starts coming down on him.)

AUGIE: Get back here. Hey Pinhead! Pinhead! I made that up! It wasn't real! But it almost worked, huh? I almost had you going, didn't I, Pinhead?

(Augie looks around, truly frightened. The door to the offstage bedroom opens and he stares into the room—what he sees in there shocks him.)

Oh my God.

(We hear the low growl of a large carnivore. It's joined by other animal sounds—growls, shrieks, the flap of wings—getting louder, sounding strange and unnatural. Augie covers his ears, knowing this is the end.)

C'mon Augie. What do you have to say now? Nothing? No apology? No remorse? No prayer? No farewell speech? No cursing? No lamentation? *(Beat)* No confession?

(Augie screams. Animal noises stop.)

Scene Eleven

Nelly enters the center room. The other rooms are dark. Nelly sits on the sofa with Johnny.

NELLY: So what do you say? Let's eat a few oranges and make wild, beautiful babies. It's been a long time, Johnny. We need to make ourselves feel good again and forget our worries. Do you want to?

JOHNNY: No.

NELLY: Are you sure?

JOHNNY: Yes.

NELLY: Never?

JOHNNY: How?

NELLY: Easy! The old-fashioned way. I take off your clothes, you take off mine, we get on top of each other—you remember.

JOHNNY: I'm too ugly.

NELLY: No!

JOHNNY: I'll make ugly babies.

NELLY: You won't make ugly babies—

JOHNNY: I'll make ugly babies! I will! I'll make ugly babies covered in scar tissue with their lips burned off and third-degree burns on their baby-blue eyes! Forget it. *(Beat)* Please forget it.

(Beat.)

NELLY: Never?

(Johnny doesn't answer.)

I'll make you change your mind. I'm not giving up. It's going to take some work, but we will have our old life back. *(She stands)* I have to go to Encino. The "Nelly and Johnny's" there is in deep trouble. They need me. I won't be long.

JOHNNY *(Sadly)*: I'm sorry about everything. Goodbye.

NELLY *(Not sure what he means)*: Goodbye? Goodbye to you.

(Nelly exits. Johnny alone.)

Scene Twelve

A red sunset washes the stage. Johnny is motionless for a moment. Then he stands.

JOHNNY: Johnny is vain. Johnny is ignorant. Johnny is perverted. Johnny is empty-headed. Johnny is self-centered. Johnny is sleazy. Johnny is redundant. Johnny is derivative.

(Johnny plucks a black orange from the tree, cuts it open and pours the cold gasoline from the orange over the furniture. Then he douses himself in the gasoline. He reaches into his pocket for a lighter, flicks on the flame and the stage is brilliant, bright red.

Johnny takes off the mask as imaginary flames engulf him. We see a projection of a burning house. As he burns:)

Nelly is good. Nelly is clever. Nelly is fierce. Nelly is loyal. Nelly is warm. Nelly is kind. Nelly is . . . Nelly is . . . is . . . is . . . is . . . is. Nelly is.

(All the areas of the stage are wrapped in flames. The light hits a bright peak and then slowly fades to black.)

Scene Thirteen

Somewhere in front of the house, Nelly runs on, on all fours—a spotlight following her. She stops in the center of the stage and looks at the audience. Hold for a moment. Then she starts running around and around, as the spotlight gets smaller and smaller. Just before it disappears, Nelly shoots to her feet as if every muscle in her body were electrified. She stands. Blackout.

CLOUD
TECTONICS

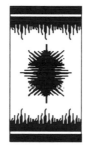

For Heather

*"Ah déjame recordarte cómo eras entonces,
cuando aún no existías."*

—*Pablo Neruda*

". . . love was the promised land,
an ark on which two might escape the Flood."

—*Julian Barnes,*

A HISTORY OF THE WORLD IN 10½ CHAPTERS

"The mystery of what a couple *is*, exactly,
is almost the only true mystery left to us,
and when we have come to the end of it
there will be no more need for literature . . ."

—*Mavis Gallant*

". . . the discovery that the speed of light appeared
the same to every observer, no matter how he was moving,
led to the theory of relativity—and in that one had to
abandon the idea that there was a unique absolute time."

—*Stephen W. Hawking,*

A BRIEF HISTORY OF TIME

"Todo me parece como un sueño todavía . . ."

—*Danny Daniel*

Cloud Tectonics received its world premiere at the 19th Annual Humana Festival of New American Plays at the Actors Theatre of Louisville (Jon Jory, Producing Director), in Louisville, Kentucky, on March 5, 1995. It was directed by Tina Landau; the set design was by Paul Owen; the costume design was by Laura Patterson; the lighting design was by T. J. Gerckens; the sound design was by Martin R. Desjardins; the fight director was Drew Fracher; the dramaturg was Michele Volansky; the stage manager was Michele Steckler; and the assistant stage manager was Janette L. Hubert. The cast was as follows:

CELESTINA DEL SOL	Camilia Sanes
ANÍBAL DE LA LUNA	Robert Montano
NELSON DE LA LUNA	Javi Mulero

Cloud Tectonics was produced by the La Jolla Playhouse (Michael Greif, Artistic Director; Terrence Dwyer, Managing Director; Robert Blacker, Associate Artistic Director) on June 20, 1995. It was directed by Tina Landau; the set design was by Riccardo Hernandez; the costume design was by Brandin Barón; the lighting design was by Anne Militello; the sound design was by Mark Bennett; the dramaturg was Gregory Gunter; and the stage manager was Kristen Harris. The cast was as follows:

CELESTINA DEL SOL	Camilia Sanes
ANÍBAL DE LA LUNA	Luis Antonio Ramos
NELSON DE LA LUNA	Javi Mulero

Cloud Tectonics was subsequently produced at Playwrights Horizons (Tim Sanford, Artistic Director) on January 5, 1997. It was directed by Tina Landau; the set design was by Riccardo Hernandez; the costume design was by Anita Yavich; the lighting design was by Frances Aronson; the sound design was by Mark Bennett and JR Conklin; the original sound score was by Mark Bennett; and the stage manager was Martha Donaldson. The cast was as follows:

CELESTINA DEL SOL	Camilia Sanes
ANÍBAL DE LA LUNA	John Ortiz
NELSON DE LA LUNA	Javi Mulero

CHARACTERS

CELESTINA DEL SOL, in her twenties.
ANÍBAL DE LA LUNA, in his thirties.
NELSON DE LA LUNA, in his twenties.

PLACE AND TIME

The Prologue
Los Angeles. The present. Night.

The Play
Same. Later that night.

The Epilogue
Same. Forty years later.

*Special thanks to Ivonne Coll
for the Spanish translation
of Celestina's speech.*

PROLOGUE

Los Angeles. Night. A bare stage with a floating bed, high in the air, tilted so the upstage headboard is slightly higher than the downstage footboard.

There is a freestanding glass wall downstage. Water drips down the side of the glass wall. It represents a city bus stop during a rainstorm. There are a pair of microphones on C-stands, downstage of the glass wall, a few feet apart.

The Prologue begins with bolero music: Los Panchos singing "Por El Amor De Una Mujer."

Celestina del Sol is standing at the bus stop. There's the sound of rain. Celestina is soaking wet. She carries a small shopping bag. She wears a thin maternity dress and she shivers. She looks exhausted, as if she's been wandering on foot for days. It's impossible to tell her actual age. It's impossible to tell if she's rich or poor. She's very, very pregnant.

As the bolero plays, Celestina holds her thumb out, hoping to catch a ride, but there doesn't seem to be any traffic in Los Angeles tonight. She reaches into a pocket, pulls out some saltine crackers and eats them hungrily, savoring each bite.

Car lights wash over Celestina. She sticks her thumb up higher. The lights cruise past her and disappear. Disappointed, Celestina eats another cracker.

We wait for the bolero to end or fade out. A moment's silence, then another car's headlights pass over Celestina. This time they stay on her. She holds her thumb up expectantly. The car's horn beckons her and she happily leaves the wall and goes to one of the microphones. The microphones are suddenly awash in red light.

Aníbal de la Luna enters and goes to the other microphone. Aníbal is a pleasant-looking man, thirties, dressed in an American Airlines ground crew uniform. Aníbal and Celestina perform the following scene into the microphones. At no time do they pantomime being in a car.

During the Prologue, Aníbal's house in the Echo Park section of Los Angeles is loaded in. This should take as long as the Prologue takes to perform.

CELESTINA *(Shivering)*: Thank you so much for this.
ANÍBAL: Jesus, you're soaked. There's a jacket in the backseat.
CELESTINA *(Putting on jacket)*: Thank you.

(Short beat.)

ANÍBAL: I can't believe anyone's out in that deluge. They're calling it the storm of the century.
CELESTINA: Where am I?
ANÍBAL: Los Angeles.
CELESTINA *(Troubled)*: Los Angeles?
ANÍBAL: Corner of Virgil and Santa Monica.
CELESTINA *(Means nothing to her)*: Oh.

(Celestina says no more. She just rubs her pregnant stomach and stares ahead. Her silence makes Aníbal a little nervous.)

ANÍBAL: Can you believe this rain for L.A.? *Coño!* Raging floods on Fairfax . . . bodies floating down the L.A. River . . . LAX closed . . . if the Big One came right now, forget it, half this city would die. But that's L.A. for you: disasters just waiting to happen.

(Aníbal laughs. No response from Celestina.)

I lived in New York. Lived in every borough except Staten Island. And Brooklyn. And Queens. And the thing is, New York kills its people one by one, you know? A gun here, a knife there, hand-to-hand combat at the ATM, little countable deaths. But this? This L.A. thing? We're talking *mass* death, *mass* destruction. One freak flood at the wrong time of year and hundreds die . . . the atmosphere sags from its own toxic heaviness and thousands perish . . . the Big One is finally born, eats a hundred thousand souls for *breakfast.* And I'm not even talking fire season!

(Celestina looks at Aníbal for the first time.)

CELESTINA: Why don't you go back to New York?
ANÍBAL: Are you kidding? I love it here. I have a house here. I have gorgeous fucking incredible-looking women falling outta the sky here! *Coño,* I've made a commitment to that!

(No response from Celestina. She eats a cracker quietly, her mind far away. Aníbal looks at her a long moment.)

You all right?
CELESTINA: The trucker that dropped me off kept touching my knees and I screamed.
ANÍBAL: How long were you out there?
CELESTINA: I don't know.
ANÍBAL: You don't know?
CELESTINA: I don't have a watch . . . I don't keep a watch . . . I don't keep "time". . . . "Time" and I don't hang out together!
ANÍBAL *(Not understanding)*: Oh. Where can I take you?
CELESTINA: I don't know.
ANÍBAL: Where were you hitching to?
CELESTINA: Nowhere. I'm not going anywhere. I don't know where I'm going, I'm sorry.
ANÍBAL: You're just out there hitching? In a hurricane? Pregnant? For fun?
CELESTINA: Are you going to ask me a lot of questions?

aníbal: Why don't I take you to a hospital? Get someone to check out your baby.

celestina: No! No! Don't do that! I don't want doctors asking me a lot of questions!

aníbal: Maybe the police could . . .

celestina: No police! Please! No police! I don't want to go to the police!

aníbal: No friends or family in L.A.?

celestina: No one. I have no one. You're the only one I have!

aníbal *(Choosing to ignore that)*: Well, you're in my car, I gotta take you somewhere . . .

celestina: Take me to this baby's father. I'm looking for this baby's father. His name is Rodrigo Cruz. Do you know him? He's a very handsome and dishonest man.

aníbal: No, I don't think I . . .

celestina: Nobody knows him. I ask everybody. That trucker took me to every state looking for Rodrigo Cruz!

aníbal: . . . I'm sorry . . .

celestina: I started my journey on Montauk Point: a room in a house, very small, my Papi sailed boats for tourists, it was some distance back—but I—I lost all track of "time"—I hate to use that word—"time"—but it's the only word I have, isn't it?

aníbal: *Coño*, I'm not following this . . .

celestina: I can give you *details* of Rodrigo Cruz. He worked for Papi repairing the boat. His eyes were ocean green. His back was wrinkled. But I can't tell you *when* he was like that, okay? He might have *changed*, you see? I can't tell you his *age*. Do you know how hard it is to find someone when you can't tell anyone their age?

aníbal: Well, it's not a problem I ever . . .

celestina: All this traveling has been a blur! It's a huge country! I never should have left my house in Montauk! I was safe in my house! Papi and Mami had it all worked out for me! They took away all the clocks!

aníbal *(Completely lost)*: The clocks?

celestina: But I was sleeping when that gorgeous son of a bitch Rodrigo Cruz came into my room! He knocked me up! He left! Now look at me! I'm starving and lost and sick of these soggy FUCKING crackers . . . and I'm just so tired of being *pregnant*!

ANÍBAL *(Worried)*: Take it easy . . .

CELESTINA: You can let me out right here, I'm sorry!

ANÍBAL: But we haven't moved. Light's still red.

CELESTINA: Please, I don't want to bother you anymore.

ANÍBAL: I don't want you sleeping outside. Not with a baby coming.

CELESTINA: I've done it before!

(The relentless rain slaps the car as Aníbal contemplates his options.)

ANÍBAL: *Coño*, okay, listen: if you promise me you're not an axe murderer . . . I promise you *I'm* not an axe murderer too, okay? You can stay in my house tonight, okay? Just tonight, okay? I'm right up here in Echo Park, okay?

CELESTINA: I can? I can't.

ANÍBAL: I promise not to touch your knees, okay?

(Celestina looks at Aníbal.)

CELESTINA: What's your name?

ANÍBAL: Oh I'm sorry. Aníbal de la Luna. Nice to meet you.

CELESTINA: I'm Celestina del Sol.

(She reaches out her hand. Aníbal and Celestina shake hands. She smiles.)

Okay. Let's go to your place.

(The light turns green. The lights go down on Aníbal and Celestina. The crew finishes assembling Aníbal's house. Aníbal and Celestina exit. The microphones are struck.)

The lights are dark in Aníbal's house, a modest pre–World War II wooden bungalow, working-class, not Hollywood.

The living room, kitchen and small eating area are basically one room full of sentimental family pictures and second- and thirdhand furniture. The door in the living room leads to the front porch. Another door leads to the bathroom. There are a couple of subtle plaster cracks in the walls from a recent earthquake.

Everything—sink, television, stereo, refrigerator, microwave, VCR, telephone, O'Keefe & Merrit stove, etc.—should be fully functional. There's a Sparkletts water dispenser in the kitchen: the bottle is empty.

The only light in the house comes from the glowing digital clocks on all the appliances. It's 8:05 P.M.

The glass wall has been incorporated into the house. Two ladders have been placed next to the floating bed to make it accessible to the living room.

We hear footsteps. The sound of keys unlocking the front door. The door opens. Suddenly all the digital clocks turn off and come back on blinking a new time: 12:00. It stays 12:00 for the rest of the scene.

Celestina and Aníbal enter from the porch. Both are dripping wet. Celestina now wears a thin suede jacket. Aníbal carries in

José Rivera

a five-gallon bottle of Sparkletts water. With the door wide open we hear distant police, ambulance and fire truck sirens. Celestina closes the door and the sirens stop.

ANÍBAL: Watch your step.
CELESTINA: It's a pretty house.
ANÍBAL: It's a craftsman. Built in the forties.
CELESTINA: Is that old?
ANÍBAL: In L.A. it's the Middle Ages.
CELESTINA *(Not understanding)*: Oh.

(Aníbal puts the water bottle on the kitchen floor as Celestina takes off the wet jacket. They both take off their waterlogged shoes.)

ANÍBAL *(Re: her shoes)*: Just leave them anywhere.
CELESTINA *(Looking around, smiles)*: I'll never forget this as long as I live.
ANÍBAL: Let me turn up the heat. Get some light going here.

(Aníbal turns up the heat and turns on some lights. Aníbal looks over at Celestina—getting his first full view of her. She's much more pregnant, and much more beautiful, than he realized. She smiles warmly at him.)

CELESTINA: You have the most beautiful house, Aníbal.
ANÍBAL: It's dry at least. More than I can say for you.

(Aníbal goes to the bathroom and comes back with a towel, which he tosses to Celestina. She dries her face, arms and feet.)

CELESTINA: You're the kindest, most beautiful man in the world! And this is the happiest night of my life!
ANÍBAL *(Smiles)*: Can I get you anything to drink?
CELESTINA *(Eager)*: Water. Please.

(Aníbal goes to the kitchen.)

ANÍBAL: So please make yourself at home. Sit. Relax.

(Aníbal puts the full Sparkletts bottle on the dispenser. He takes the empty bottle out to the porch: again, as he opens the door, we hear distant sirens, which stop when he closes the door.

Too happy to sit still, Celestina starts exploring the house, checking out pictures on tables, books on bookshelves, etc.)

CELESTINA: Everything is so beautiful. Everything in order.

ANÍBAL: Debbie does that.

CELESTINA: My little room in Montauk had no order. It wasn't big, but it was my whole world. Things were everywhere, on top of everything: I'd sleep in my clothes, and eat in bed, and read detective novels, hardly ever sleep, dream wide-awake, make plans that were never fulfilled, watch storms coming in, laugh at the moon's neurotic phases, hear stars being scraped across the sky, dance, sing boleros, make love to myself over and over, live a whole life in one room!

(Celestina laughs as she holds herself and does a little dance around the room.)

ANÍBAL *(Giving her a look)*: You want a quesadilla?

CELESTINA: And my Mami and Papi worked so hard for me. They loved me so much. They thought I was cursed! They really did! They put everything in its proper place for me!

(Aníbal looks at Celestina a long moment, not sure what to make of all this.)

ANÍBAL: Your parents thought you were cursed?

CELESTINA: Yeah. They're dead. I'd love a quesadilla.

ANÍBAL: Wait.

CELESTINA: Papi used to cross himself when he looked at me. Mami wouldn't breast-feed me. They kept eighteen statues of Jesus Christ in my room!

ANÍBAL: Wait. Why did you live in one room . . . ?

(Celestina looks at Aníbal, aware of his look. She laughs.)

CELESTINA: I'm not a lunatic. Hey. You're in no danger, stranger. It's just hard for me to tell a story. Straight.

ANÍBAL *(Worried about her baby)*: Just take it easy. For both of you.

CELESTINA *(Touching her stomach)*: This baby must think I'm a lunatic too!

ANÍBAL: But I don't—

CELESTINA: I wonder what this baby hears. Oh God! This baby must've heard me talking to that trucker, and all his dirty words! Ugly, filthy man!

(Celestina suddenly gets a fierce contraction that doubles her over. Aníbal goes to her and takes her hand.)

ANÍBAL: Celestina, please . . . if you . . . if you sat down, I'd feel a lot better . . .

CELESTINA *(Pain)*: Why?

ANÍBAL: 'Cause if you get too agitated, you might . . . I mean, I don't want you having that baby all over my floor tonight . . .

CELESTINA: And your floor is so clean!

ANÍBAL: Yes . . . I mean, you're not, like, *coño, due* tonight, are you?

CELESTINA *(Pain subsiding)*: I don't know.

ANÍBAL: You don't know?

(The discomfort goes away and Celestina straightens up again. She smiles as if nothing happened.)

CELESTINA: I don't think so.

ANÍBAL: Well, wait. How pregnant are you? Exactly.

CELESTINA *(Defensive)*: What do you mean?

ANÍBAL: How far along are you?

CELESTINA: I'm not really sure.

ANÍBAL: You're not *sure?*

CELESTINA: This is the warmest, most enchanting house I've ever . . .

ANÍBAL: Wait. Isn't knowing how pregnant you are . . . a little basic? Like knowing your age?

CELESTINA: Yes . . . yes it is . . . but you should never ask a woman's age, you might not like what you hear! *(Smiles at him)* Can I have my water?

(Aníbal looks at Celestina, then goes to the Sparkletts dispenser and pours Celestina a tall glass of water. He gives it to her.

Celestina drinks the water very fast, almost choking on it, like she hasn't had water in a long time. Finished, she holds out her empty glass for more. As Aníbal takes Celestina's empty glass and goes back for a refill, Celestina finds a framed picture of a young woman on a table.)

CELESTINA: So do you have a lot of "gorgeous fucking incredible-looking women" in your life, Aníbal?

(Aníbal hands Celestina the glass of water.)

ANÍBAL *(Re: photograph)*: Well, no. Well, one. That one.

CELESTINA: She's beautiful.

ANÍBAL: That's Debbie.

(Celestina looks at the photograph a long time. Aníbal waits for her to say something.)

She's at her office now. She sleeps there a lot. She works for Disney. She answers phones. She's gorgeous. She's Puerto Rican too but she changed her name from Epifania Niguayona Gonzalez to Debbie Shapiro. They still don't respect her. She thinks they do. But she's deluding herself. I can tell. I know guys. I know when a guy is thinking pussy and every guy she works with at Disney is thinking pussy. She thinks they're thinking brain cells. They're not going to make her an executive like she thinks. She's going to remain a receptionist until she turns thirty, then they're gonna fire her and get a younger, prettier, whiter-looking Latin girl to replace her.

CELESTINA: Will she mind my being here?

ANÍBAL: She'd hate it except you're pregnant. Deb doesn't believe in friendship between the sexes, she believes in sex between the sexes. Being pregnant makes you safe.

CELESTINA *(Surprised)*: I'm safe?

ANÍBAL: Guess so.

(Celestina puts the photograph down, finishes her glass of water and looks at Aníbal.)

CELESTINA: What do you believe? Sex or friendship?

ANÍBAL: I believe friendship between the sexes is not only possible, it's preferable. Makes everything cleaner. But then I don't work in the movie business. I load luggage at LAX. There's no sex in that job.

CELESTINA *(Shocked)*: None?

(Beat. Aníbal isn't sure how far he wants this conversation to go, but there's something about Celestina. He can't help but open up to her.)

ANÍBAL: The closest is . . . I look up at an airplane sometimes and it's full of people going to New York and sometimes I make eye contact with a woman at a window seat in first class. And she's looking down at me, daydreaming, maybe she's afraid of the flight, thinking this could be her last hour on earth, wondering if she's done enough, dared enough, eaten enough, and everyone around her seems dead already. And that fear of crashing is bringing all her latent sexual dreams up from their deep well, and she's getting all excited by her own images—and there *we* are, making split-second eye contact and suddenly that faceless male in her dream world has a pair of eyes . . . and they are vivid eyes, and they are Puerto Rican eyes, and they are my eyes, Celestina.

(A short silence. Celestina goes to Aníbal. She gets close to him—so close her huge belly gently touches his stomach. She looks into Aníbal's eyes. The intensity of this makes Aníbal a little nervous.)

What are you doing?

CELESTINA: Can I see?

ANÍBAL: Can you see? What? Can you what?

CELESTINA: Your vivid, Puerto Rican eyes, Aníbal, can I see them?

ANÍBAL *(Nervous)*: Why? No.

CELESTINA: Just because. Let me.

ANÍBAL: *Coño*, I brought you here on faith, now. That you're not a killer. Not a psycho. Not a hypnotizing, blood-drinking Scientologist . . .

(Celestina looks deep into Aníbal's eyes.)

CELESTINA: I think about sex all the time, though I've only had one lover in my life, only one time. Rodrigo Cruz. And I almost had two! That despicable trucker who kept touching my knees. But I ran away from him. I took my chances in the rain. But even he couldn't stop my endless daydreaming and nightdreaming about sex: about Rodrigo's wrinkled back, my legs wrapped around his face . . . this obsession of mine . . . this tidal wave that started sometime when I was younger, when I lived in that one room. When Papi bought me a bicycle to give me something else to think about besides my body, and one glorious day I was allowed to ride around and around the house, because my Papi wanted me to count numbers, count numbers, over and over; he said it would teach me about the nature of "time," and I tried and tried, I really did, but I didn't learn anything, I was just so grateful to be outside my little room for once! *(Beat)*

Then Papi hired Rodrigo to work on his boat "The Celestina." And I would stare at him from my window as he worked. He was beautiful. I wondered if I was in love. And he would look back at me and stare and his hair was so long and black. And I wondered is that what love looks like? And I don't know how many years passed . . . (I didn't know the word "years" then. I learned it on the road when the trucker taught me all kinds of words like "years" and "now" and "yesterday" and "minute" and "century") . . . and it must have been years . . . because years are longer than days (I learned this!) . . . and Rodrigo's hair was long and gray and he snuck into my room and did his dirty thing and left me . . . and my parents died in the other room and I went out to see because the house had grown so quiet and there they were in their little bed, holding hands, the green bedspread half covering their wrinkled bodies, they were naked and pale and covered in long gray hairs and very, very dead. That's the one time I stopped dreaming of sex when I called the police and told them Mami and Papi were dead, then I got dressed, and I lost all track of "time" and I got scared, and I ran out into the rain because I was sure they'd blame me and in my endless stay in my one room I didn't learn much, but I learned by reading detective novels that when somebody dies the police always come to take you away and kill you with a lightning chair. That's when I hit the road, pregnant, looking for Rodrigo Cruz, angry and excited because he was the only man I ever had sex with and I keep thinking about sex with Rodrigo and I love the word "sex" and if I could fuck fuck fuck all day I would!

(Aníbal impulsively, quickly, kisses Celestina. She gasps. Aníbal turns away.)

ANÍBAL: Let me start those quesadillas for you!

(Aníbal quickly turns on the griddle and busies himself in the kitchen.)

CELESTINA: I should leave.

(Celestina starts to go to the front door.)

ANÍBAL: I don't want you to leave.
CELESTINA: You don't think I'm strange?
ANÍBAL: I do think you're strange. But I don't want you to leave.
CELESTINA: But I don't know how long I've been here. I don't know if it's been too long! I should go!
ANÍBAL *(Re: the kiss)*: I'm sorry I did that! I never do that!

CELESTINA: Have I been here minutes? Days?! Shit! I knew this would happen!

ANÍBAL: A half hour at the most! Twenty minutes. Not days.

CELESTINA: Are you sure?

(Aníbal looks at his watch.)

ANÍBAL: My watch stopped.

CELESTINA *(Knew this would happen)*: I really have to go before Rodrigo turns into an unrecognizable old man and dies!

(Aníbal looks at all the digital clocks in the house—all are blinking 12:00.)

ANÍBAL: The clocks have stopped . . .

(Celestina goes to put on her shoes and the wet jacket.)

CELESTINA: I can't miss my chance to make that bastard do right by me!

(Celestina goes to the door, opens it. We hear sirens. Aníbal grabs Celestina's arm, physically stopping her from running out.)

ANÍBAL: Celestina, wait a second—

CELESTINA: *I can't wait a second; I don't know what you mean!*

ANÍBAL: You've been here only a few *minutes*. Just minutes. Tomorrow morning, when the sun comes up, it'll be only a few *hours* . . .

(Beat. She looks at him.)

CELESTINA: Hours? Is it a lot?

ANÍBAL: *Coño* . . . I think something has happened to you, Celestina, some kind of trauma, and you're not making any *sense* . . .

CELESTINA *(Offended)*: I have not lost my mind.

ANÍBAL: Please. Eat dinner. Sleep on the sofa bed. In the morning, we'll have a big breakfast and I'll give you some money.
Drive you wherever you want, okay?

*(Aníbal goes to the kitchen and comes back with another glass of
water. He holds it out for Celestina. Still thirsty, Celestina comes
back in and takes the glass of water.)*

CELESTINA: Your beauty is overwhelming, Aníbal.

*(Aníbal closes the door. The sirens stop. Celestina takes off her
shoes and the jacket.*
    *Keeping a watchful eye on Celestina as she drinks the water,
Aníbal goes to the kitchen, opens the refrigerator and takes out
packets of tortillas, cheese, salsa and guacamole. As Aníbal prepares dinner, he can't help but look at her in wonder.)*

ANÍBAL: Who are you, Celestina?

*(Celestina smiles at the inevitable question, then thinks a
moment. She starts setting the table for dinner as Aníbal puts the
tortillas and cheese on the hot griddle.)*

CELESTINA: How do you know what "time" feels like, Aníbal?

(Aníbal looks at her a second.)

In your body? You feel it, don't you? Pushing at your heart
muscles. Pricking the nerves in your brain. Turning some on,
turning some off. Is that what "time" feels like? And where *is*
"time"? Is the organ for "time" the heart? Is it the spinal
chord, that silver waterfall of nerves and memories: is "time"
in there? Is it the gonads? Does "time" have a sound? What
bells, Aníbal, what vibrating string played by what virtuoso
accompanies the passage of "time"? Is "time" blue? Does it
taste like steak? Can you fuck it? Or is it just the invisible
freight train that runs you over every single day . . . breaking
you into smaller and smaller pieces . . . pieces so small they

can't hold your soul to the earth anymore, and *that's* why you die? C'mon, Aníbal, help me out here!

ANÍBAL: We just know. Common sense tells us.

CELESTINA: Well, then . . . what if there are people born who don't have that sense? Don't have that inner clock telling them when a moment has passed, when another has started, how a day feels different from a year. What would you say to such people?

ANÍBAL: *Coño:* your imagination . . .

CELESTINA: And what if these people don't progress through space and "time" the same way you do? They don't age smoothly. They stay little far longer than they should. Or the rhythms of the day mean nothing. So they sleep for weeks at a "time." They stay awake all winter scaring the shit out of their parents! They can make love for two weeks straight without a break!

ANÍBAL: I don't know.

(Beat.)

CELESTINA: No. Of course not. How could you?

(Dinner is ready. The table is set. Celestina looks at the table appreciatively.)

I should wash my hands.

ANÍBAL *(Re: the bathroom)*: That way.

(Celestina starts to go off. Then she looks at Aníbal. She goes to him, kisses him on the cheek and embraces him. He holds her close.)

CELESTINA: Papi told me he was twenty-five when I was born. Before he died, we celebrated his seventy-ninth birthday. When the trucker picked me up outside of Montauk Point, I was pregnant and starting to show. When we crossed the frontier into Los Angeles, before he touched my knees, he put two candles on a little cake and said we were celebrating two years together. *(Beat)* So that's who I am: I'm a fifty-four-year-old woman, Aníbal, and I've been pregnant with this baby for two years.

(Celestina goes to the bathroom and closes the door. Aníbal is alone. Aníbal goes to the telephone in the living room. Picks it up. It's dead. Aníbal slams it down.)

ANÍBAL: Shit.

(Aníbal goes to the TV and turns it on. All he can get, channel after channel, is static. He turns on a radio. More static.
Aníbal goes back to the kitchen and hides all the knives. There's a knock at the door. Aníbal looks at the door, worried. A second knock. Aníbal goes to the door and opens it. Sirens.
Aníbal's younger brother, Sergeant Nelson de la Luna, is there. Nelson, twenty-five, is taller, broader than his older brother: he has a sweet baby face, short hair and a little mustache. Nelson wears an army-issue raincoat and army boots.)

Nelson?

NELSON *(Big smile)*: Brother!

(Nelson laughs and scoops up Aníbal in a big bear hug. The brothers kiss and pound each other's backs.)

ANÍBAL: Son of a bitch, Nelson, what the fuck are you doing here?!

NELSON: Surprise! Nice *house*!

(Nelson comes in, takes off his raincoat. Underneath he wears army-issue T-shirt, khakis, dog tags, etc. Aníbal still can't believe his brother's there. He closes the door. Sirens stop.)

ANÍBAL: Look at you. Fucking amazing. Are you alone?

NELSON: No, I got half the company out in the Grand National, asshole. Man look at you. You old.

ANÍBAL: Fuck you too. What an asshole; didn't even *call* me . . .

NELSON: Surprise, surprise, how much you pay for this dump?

ANÍBAL: What a dickhead! So what's up? I thought you were in Germany.

NELSON: Not anymore, bro. They shipped my ass to Fort Benning, Georgia, six months ago. Then they sent my ass out here for two days.

ANÍBAL: Are you in training for something? Getting ready to invade some hapless Third World country?

NELSON: "Hapless." What a homo. You got a beer?

(Nelson goes to the refrigerator and helps himself to a beer.)

ANÍBAL: Have a beer.

NELSON: I'm fucking out in Death Valley now. It's a fucking *lake.* I thought you lived in sunny Southern California, jerk-off.

ANÍBAL: It rains out here too, asswipe. *Coño,* it's great to see you, Nelson.

(They embrace exuberantly again, pound backs.)

NELSON: So yeah, got my ass shipped to Death Valley, I'm good to go, bro, desert training for the Middle East or some towel-head shithole with oil underneath it . . . fucking tanks all over the place, blow up anything stupid enough to get in our way—mostly stray sheep and coyotes—'cause we're *men,* Aníbal, not pussies like you: men, MEN!

ANÍBAL *(Laughs)*: Get outta my face with that shit.

NELSON: Yo, it beats jerkin' off all day like you, so this is your *house* finally, I gotta get me one of these, I guess loading luggage really pays, what: you helpin' smuggle drugs 'n' shit?

ANÍBAL *(Laughs)*: How long are you staying?

NELSON: Man, I'm hosed. I gotta be back in Death Valley oh-five-hundred tomorrow morning for a fucking dipshit meeting with my C.O. that's only supposed to last five *minutes.* So I can only hang 'bout an hour, 'cause the roads suck tonight.

ANÍBAL *(Disappointed)*: An hour? Nelson, I haven't seen you in six years.

NELSON: Time flies, motherfucker!

ANÍBAL: So why can't you call the guy—?
NELSON: No way. Gotta *be* there. They gotta *see* my ass in front of the C.O., in person. It's really fucking stupid.
ANÍBAL: The army's perfect for you.
NELSON *(Re: Aníbal)*: What a waste of a human being. Man, you get uglier and stupider all the time.
ANÍBAL: You're just pissed my mother loved me and she didn't love you.

(Nelson starts looking for the bathroom.)

NELSON: Aw shit, where's the head, man? All I've eaten is beef jerky and I gotta take a massive dump.
ANÍBAL: You're a poet, Nelson, you know that? A poet of our time.
NELSON: Yo, eat me!
ANÍBAL: There's somebody in the bathroom. A woman.
NELSON *(Surprised)*: You got a woman in your bathroom, Aníbal?
ANÍBAL: Her name is Celestina. I picked her up tonight.
NELSON *(Big smile)*: Brother! You're *not* a total waste!

(Nelson high-fives Aníbal.)

ANÍBAL: No, she's pregnant, Nelson, and she's . . . I think . . . mentally disturbed or something . . . or she's living in a dream world, I don't know.
NELSON: Women.
ANÍBAL: She looks like she's twenty-five years old but she *says* she's fifty-four.
NELSON: That's fucking L.A., bro.
ANÍBAL: And she says she's been pregnant for two years.
NELSON: And you picked her up? *You're* not an asshole!
ANÍBAL: She was hitching. In this storm. I can't drive by somebody like that.
NELSON: A total fairy. What a liberal. Is she cute?
ANÍBAL: She's gorgeous.
NELSON: Oh well, that's cool. I could fuck an insane pregnant girl if she's gorgeous.
ANÍBAL: Don't be a pig, Nelson—

NELSON: What? I'll have that bitch howlin' at the moon!

ANÍBAL: She's not—

NELSON: Hey, I've been in a *tank* nine *weeks*, bro, I'm ready to seduce *goats*. Swear: my mother must've been exposed to radiation when you were born.

ANÍBAL *(Laughs)*: Fuck you through the head.

NELSON: *You're* the fucking poet of our time! Asshole! Liberal! I'mma fuckin' body slam you!

(Nelson lunges at Aníbal. Aníbal fights him off. They wrestle around the living room, knocking furniture around, laughing. Nelson catches Aníbal.

Nelson lifts Aníbal over his head and prepares to body slam him.)

ANÍBAL: Nelson—*DOOOOOOON'T*!!

(Celestina comes in. She's got a gun. She aims it at Nelson's head. Both men freeze.)

NELSON: Oh shit.

ANÍBAL: Celestina . . . ?

NELSON *(Already admiring her)*: Training and instinct tell me that's a gun.

CELESTINA: Put him down.

(Nelson quickly puts Aníbal down. Celestina continues pointing the gun at Nelson.)

ANÍBAL: Celestina. Could you please put that away—it's fine . . .

CELESTINA: Who is he?

ANÍBAL: —this is my brother—Nelson—this is Nelson, it's okay . . .

(Celestina reluctantly puts the gun in a pocket. Both men are greatly relieved. Nelson laughs nervously.)

NELSON: Whoa. Fuckme. I love L.A.!

ANÍBAL: I didn't know you were armed, Celestina. *Christ.*

CELESTINA: I stole it from the trucker while he was sleeping.

NELSON: Whoa.

ANÍBAL *(Still shaken)*: Jesus.

CELESTINA: I'm sorry, Aníbal, I . . .

ANÍBAL: It's cool. It's just—*coño.* Heart attack.

CELESTINA: I wanted to protect you.

NELSON *(To Aníbal)*: She wanted to protect you, asshole!

ANÍBAL *(To Nelson)*: I'm not crazy about guns.

NELSON *(To Celestina)*: I am. *(Sotto to Aníbal)* She's gorgeous, man. Introduce.

ANÍBAL *(Wary)*: Fuck. Nelson, this is Celestina. Celestina, this is my little brother, Nelson.

(Celestina goes to shake Nelson's hand.)

CELESTINA *(To Nelson)*: Nice to meet you.

NELSON *(Big charming smile)*: So Celestina, what's *up*?!

ANÍBAL *(Sotto to Nelson)*: Nelson . . . slow . . .

NELSON *(Sotto to Aníbal)*: Step back or I'll body slam you . . .

ANÍBAL *(Sotto to Nelson; re: Celestina)*: . . . disturbed . . . ?

NELSON *(To Celestina)*: . . . I'm married, okay? But. I'm separated from my wife. Bitch left me. Got drunk one night, said: "You know, Nelson, deep inside o' my heart, I just don't like you fucking little greasy Puerto Ricans!" I said, "Fuck you, 'ho" and threw a hand grenade at her.

CELESTINA *(Amused)*: You threw a hand grenade . . . ?

ANÍBAL *(Horrified)*: You threw a hand grenade . . . ?

NELSON *(Defensive)*: It didn't go off! We filed for divorce. That little baby got a father?

CELESTINA: I'm looking for him. His name is Rodrigo Cruz.

NELSON: You married to him?

CELESTINA: No but I'm going to make him!

NELSON: You love this man?

CELESTINA: I don't know.

NELSON: Well, if you don't find him, let me know. I love children. I understand children. You have beautiful eyes, Celestina.

CELESTINA: Thank you.

ANÍBAL: I may vomit.

NELSON: I can't stay too long, Celestina. I'm serving our country in the armed forces of the U.S. Protecting us from . . . uhm . . . not communists . . . uhm . . . illegal aliens, drug kingpins and Arabs. It's dangerous work. My life is on the line each and every day. But I'm good to go! And the thing is, I gotta be back in Death Valley tonight—*Death* Valley, so appropriate, huh?—I have very important meetings with high-ranking officers—then I go to Fort Benning, Georgia, Monday to finalize my divorce from my cracker wife. And then, in about two years, I'll be getting my discharge from the army. What I'm saying is . . . I won't be back this way for a while. But I'm gonna come back in two years and look you up, okay? And if you ain't found that baby's father, I just might ask you to marry me, 'cause no woman should raise her baby alone. You understand? This cool with you, Celestina? Can I ask you?

CELESTINA *(Not knowing what to say)*: Uhm. You can ask me.

NELSON: Yes! Good! Well, my work is done here. Bye.

(Nelson goes to his raincoat and starts putting it on.)

ANÍBAL: What do you mean? What are you doing?

NELSON: I gotta get back to Death Valley. Duty calls.

ANÍBAL: Right *now!*

NELSON *(Looking at his watch)*: No! My watch died! Fuckit. Yes. I gotta go. I'll take my dump on the road. I'm fucked I'm not there.

ANÍBAL: This is happening too fast —

NELSON: What's life? A fucking *blink.* Get used to it. And thanks for introducing me to the woman of my dreams, homeboy.

(Celestina smiles. Then she gets another pain in her belly.)

CELESTINA: Ohhhhhhhh.

(Nelson and Aníbal quickly go to Celestina.)

ANÍBAL AND NELSON: You okay??

CELESTINA *(Still in pain)*: It's okay. Thank you. *(Another jolt)* Why is my baby doing this? Why is he tapping my spine with his fingers? What code is that? What words?

(Nelson looks at her pregnant stomach.)

NELSON: May I?

(Celestina nods yes and Nelson kneels at her feet and rubs her belly. The pain slowly subsides. Celestina smiles with relief.)

CELESTINA: Thank you, Nelson.

(Nelson puts his head on her stomach, listening to the sounds inside.)

NELSON: Check it out. I can hear the ocean! Stars being scraped across the sky!

CELESTINA *(Delighted)*: You can?

NELSON: I hear a little body searching for the way out. Little bones. *(To her stomach)* Yo in there. I'mma wait for you, little man. Be the father of your dreams. You come outta this deep night you're in, *hijo de mi alma*, see my big-ass smile, you're gonna know what sunshine is! That cool? And you tell your beautiful mami to wait for me, okay *mijo*?

(Nelson kisses Celestina's stomach. Moved, Celestina gently kisses the top of Nelson's head.
Nelson gets up. Nelson and Aníbal have a long embrace.)

ANÍBAL: Six years, Nelson. Six fucking years.

NELSON: This is the happiest night of my life!

(Nelson opens the door. Sirens. He disappears into the rain. Aníbal goes to the door.)

ANÍBAL: You'll never get to Death Valley in that rain . . .

NELSON *(Off)*: A *man* would!

(Aníbal watches Nelson driving away, his back to the audience. Aníbal sadly waves goodbye. Celestina looks at Aníbal. Aníbal closes the door. Sirens stop.
Celestina is watching Aníbal, who is quiet a long moment, his mind far away.)

CELESTINA: You okay?

(Beat. He tries to smile. He starts clearing up the kitchen table.)

ANÍBAL: Are you really going to wait for him? Two years?
CELESTINA: I don't know what "two years" means, Aníbal.

(Aníbal rubs his tired eyes—then looks at his watch—then realizes it's not working.)

ANÍBAL: I don't even know what time it is. It could be next week. I don't remember this morning. I don't remember kissing Debbie goodbye or working or eating or driving from LAX or finding a hitchhiker in the storm of the century. And was my fucking little *brother* really here? I can't believe he's a *man* already! Ten minutes ago, *I* was body slamming *him*!
CELESTINA: Why don't we eat?
ANÍBAL *(Trying to focus)*: Eat. Yeah. Eat.

(Aníbal and Celestina sit at the kitchen table. Celestina can hardly wait and immediately stuffs her mouth with food, eating with the passion of a starving person.)

CELESTINA *(Mouth full)*: This is the best food!
ANÍBAL *(Concerned)*: Easy . . . Celestina . . . easy . . .

(Aníbal and Celestina continue their dinner. This should take it's natural time—despite the speed with which Celestina attacks her food—and should happen in silence.
All the while Aníbal and Celestina may make periodic eye

*contact—smile—look away—sometimes Aníbal finds himself
staring—sometimes Celestina does.*
    *Suddenly the house is rocked by several claps of harsh thun-
der. The lightning outside lights up the house through the windows brighter than could possibly occur in nature.*
    Celestina looks at Aníbal.)

CELESTINA: *Me pregunto . . . me pregunto como será haberte amado
en cada etapa de tu vida, Aníbal.*

(Beat. He looks at her and she continues in Spanish.)

*Amar al niñito que fuiste, y tomarte de la mano, y ayudarte a
cruzar la calle, y besar tu barriguita gordita de bebé, y peinar
tus greñitas de chiquillo. Y luego, mas adelante, amar al anciano
en que te convertiste, y besar tus arrugas profundas, y suavizar
tu pelo canoso, y deleitar tu sabio y cansado corazón, y mirar
fijamente hacia adentro de esos ojos misteriosos, mas alla de las
cataratas, y muy adentro de tí, hacia los verdes prados donde uno
nunca envejece. ¿No te pareceria lindo tener ese tipo de amor,
Aníbal? ¿El amor de toda una vida?*

(Beat. Aníbal smiles nervously.)

ANÍBAL: What?
CELESTINA: What?
ANÍBAL: I didn't know you could speak Spanish.
CELESTINA *(Smiles)*: *Solamente hablo Español cuando estoy
enamorada.*
ANÍBAL: What?

(Beat.)

CELESTINA: Don't you speak *any* Spanish?
ANÍBAL *(Sad)*: I don't.
CELESTINA: You don't?
ANÍBAL: I don't.
CELESTINA: Why not?

ANÍBAL: Sometimes . . . I don't know . . . you forget things . . .

CELESTINA: But how do you forget a *language?*

ANÍBAL: It happened, Celestina. It's not nice and I'm not proud of it, but it happened.

CELESTINA: I'm sorry.

ANÍBAL: All I know is "*coño!*"

CELESTINA *(Laughs)*: Well, "*coño*"'s useful.

(Celestina laughs sadly. Aníbal laughs with her. He looks at her. She reaches out a hand. He takes it and holds it a moment.)

ANÍBAL *(Pulling away)*: I'll get the sofa bed ready for you.

(Beat.)

CELESTINA: Okay. I'll help you set up.

(During the following speech, Aníbal goes to the sofa bed, pulls it out. He goes to the closet and comes back with pillows, blankets and sheets. Together he and Celestina make the sofa bed. If necessary for timing, Aníbal could go through whatever bedtime ritual he needs: turning off lights, locking the door, turning on the security system, taking out the trash, etc.

Toward the end of the speech, while Aníbal is deeper in his memories, he stops looking at Celestina. Behind Aníbal, facing upstage, Celestina takes off her maternity dress and slips into a nightgown she keeps in her shopping bag. She lets her long hair down. She looks more unearthly, more angelic than ever.)

ANÍBAL: I made love with Debbie just last night. Or was it this morning? *(Beat)* I had to talk her into spending the night, instead of sleeping in her office again. It seems like a million years ago. *(Beat)* I know Debbie from high school in the Bronx. We went out. Then she went out of state for college and I couldn't afford college so I stayed behind and worked. She married her English professor and moved to Ohio. I wanted to kill myself. I spent the next five years getting into these other relationships. The first one, I was twenty-two.

The woman I fell in love with was thirty-nine. We had a great time together. But I took her home to meet my parents and my father made a pass at her and it was over. Then I fell in love with a blonde. She was a real beauty. But she came from this fucked-up home and she had a drug problem and she drank too much and the night I told her I didn't love her anymore she tried to throw herself out of a moving car on the Belt Parkway. Then I fell in love with a series of lesbians. Every woman I liked turned out to be gay! Then one night, New Year's Eve, I'm living in the Lower East Side, the phone rings, it's Debbie. She left her husband. She left Ohio. She was staying at her sister's in Harlem. Would I like to get together. *(Beat)* I went to her place. I didn't know what to expect. She was staying in one of those worn-out tenements with the steam heat up too high and the steel radiators that clamored all night, and Willie Colón and laughing and partying and loud kissing coming at you from all the apartments all over us. People just exploding! Going nuts! I remember the smell of *tos—tos—*

CELESTINA: *Tostones!*

ANÍBAL: *Tostones!* And rice and beans and *lechón—lechón—*

CELESTINA: *Lechón asado!*

ANÍBAL: *Lechón asado!* You know: everything cooked with a lot of *man—*

CELESTINA: *Manteca!*

ANÍBAL: *Manteca!* And I held Debbie all night long. We didn't fuck. I kissed her a lot. We touched all over. But we didn't go to bed. We were starting over. I was figuring out this new body. She seemed richer. All the years we hadn't seen each other, miles she's traveled, all this married wisdom and experience she had that I didn't have. I felt like a *boy*, a child, in the arms of this mature *woman*. We decided that night to go to Los Angeles together and start over. Be in that one city where you can really remake yourself. Pan for gold in the L.A. River. She wanted to get rich on the movies. I wanted to get away from the racists who thought of me only as a spik. *(Beat)*

As we were holding each other, touching each other, I

started to remember something I thought I had forgotten. It was when I was a little boy. I don't even remember how old. We were living in Newark, New Jersey. We were visiting my cousins who lived in a big house in Patchogue, Long Island. My child's memory makes that house enormous, like a Victorian haunted house, but maybe it wasn't. They had thirteen kids. We used to watch *lucha libre* together, professional wrestling, all the time. One time my cousin Ernesto got carried away watching Bruno San Martino on TV and he punched me in the stomach. Ernie liked to inflict pain. He had long, black curly hair and a thin black mustache, freckles, large, red lips, crooked teeth: he was the cousin that looked most like me. Another night, after a party, my cousin Cheo told me how he could feel his balls flapping around in his pants when he danced to American music. He balls went flap-flap-flap when he danced to rock 'n' roll. I liked Cheo. He never punched me like Ernesto did. Cheo taught me about exponents and square roots. He went to Vietnam. Everybody thought Ernesto would get into drug dealing. *(Beat)*

One night I was on the second floor of my cousins' house. I remember walking past a dark bedroom: the door was open. I thought I heard a voice inside calling my name. I went in. My cousin Eva was there. She was older than Ernie or Cheo. Much older than me. I remember her standing by the window. I could see her face lit up by a streetlight—or was it the moon? I remember there was a heavy smell in the room. And I don't know how I eventually got there . . . but I ended up lying in bed with Eva. I was on my back, looking at the ceiling. Eva was kneeling next to me. Then Eva lifted her dress and she was straddling me and pressing her pelvis into me. I think she had her underwear on. I had my pants on and I didn't know why she was doing this to me, though I knew I had to do this because she was my older cousin, therefore she had authority. I remember her legs being smooth. I remember her face. She was looking out the window. I don't remember how long this lasted. I don't remember if anyone came in. I don't remember if anyone ever knew about this, though, later on it seemed that everybody knew. I liked Eva on top of me. I remember her weight. I liked her weight. I don't remember if I got hard or not: I was only a little boy! I liked watching Eva's face, the way she looked out the window. How the light struck half her face. I wish I could remember her mouth! I think it was open. But I don't remember. Was there a smile? Did she bite her lower lip? Was she talking to me? Did she say something in Spanish? I remember her eyes. *(Beat)*

So I fell in love with Eva. She was all I thought about. And I think my mother suspected something and she was worried about us, though first cousins had married several times in my family. One night my mother and I were washing dishes together, side by side. And we had the only conversation about sex we were ever to have. Without looking at me, she said: "Aníbal, remember: there is some fruit you are not allowed to eat." And that's all she said. And I knew *exactly* what she meant. And it was all she had to say to me. *(Beat)*

I've never forgotten Eva. Even in Debbie's arms after five years of missing her and wanting her, I thought easily of Eva. It's like . . . the space around my body was permanently curved—or dented—by Eva's heaviness. I wonder if love sometimes does that to you. It alters the physics around you in some way: changing the speed of light and the shape of space and how you experience time.

CELESTINA: What do you think made you fall in love with those women?

ANÍBAL: Do you think I know?

(Aníbal turns around to look at Celestina, who has changed into her nightgown. She smiles at him. Beat.)

CELESTINA: Would you rub my feet?

ANÍBAL: What?

CELESTINA: Would you rub my feet? They're freezing.

(Beat.)

ANÍBAL: Uhm, sure.

(Beat. Celestina sits on the sofa bed and puts her bare feet up expectantly. Aníbal sits with her, her feet on his lap. He gently rubs her feet. She closes her eyes in bliss.)

CELESTINA: Hmmmmmm . . . yeah . . .

(Celestina seems to fall asleep, a look of peace and serenity on her face. Aníbal looks at her a moment and can't help but smile.)

ANÍBAL: *Buenas noches.*

(Aníbal starts to get up. Celestina opens her eyes.)

CELESTINA: Kiss my toes.
ANÍBAL: . . . What?
CELESTINA: Just once?
ANÍBAL: Kiss your—what—?
CELESTINA: Please? Just once?

(Beat.)

ANÍBAL: Okay.

(Aníbal kisses her toes one by one. She smiles with each little kiss, trying not to giggle, eyes still closed.
Aníbal finishes and starts to leave.)

CELESTINA: No you don't.
ANÍBAL: Now what?
CELESTINA: Higher.
ANÍBAL: . . . Higher?
CELESTINA: Up the body.
ANÍBAL: Okay.

(Aníbal kisses her knees. Celestina sighs deeply, stretching out.)

CELESTINA: Little higher.

(Aníbal kisses her thighs. Celestina whispers.)

Up.

(Aníbal kisses her enormous stomach.)

More up.

(Aníbal kisses her breasts.)

Keep going.

(Aníbal kisses her neck.)

. . . Home, traveler. You're home!

(Aníbal kisses Celestina lightly once on the lips. They hold each other a long moment. We hear the sound of the rain beating against the house. They don't look at each other as they talk.)

ANÍBAL: I'm afraid.
CELESTINA: Don't be.
ANÍBAL: Not about bodies. I'm afraid we're going to be mixing my sad dreams with your wild ones.
CELESTINA *(Smiles)*: Maybe they'll have beautiful children, Aníbal.

(Aníbal kisses her gently on the lips. She opens her mouth to him and takes him in, kissing him back with all the passion in her body.)

ANÍBAL: Celestina.

(Celestina speaks to Aníbal as she holds him.)

CELESTINA: I'm a stranger in my own body, Aníbal. A stranger to my own past. My memories don't make sense to me. I doubt everything. I don't even believe what people verify for me. I even wonder if my real name is Celestina del Sol! *(Beat)* Sometimes you're with somebody and you don't seem so strange to yourself anymore. Somehow, by luck or chemistry or divine intervention or insanity, you collide with another life, and there's an explosion followed by peace. For a second, a year, fifty years—whatever those things mean—you feel you've reached some kind of home. Sometimes there's no "time"—only an endless now that needs to be filled with life. To be rescued from habit and death. *(Beat)* C'mon.

ANÍBAL: Okay.

(Aníbal takes Celestina's hand and leads her to the ladders which go up to the floating bed.

As they climb the ladders, the rest of the house seems to disappear and be replaced by vague twinkling stars and crescent moons and dark, silvery clouds.

As they reach the bed, there's another knock at the door.

The house instantly changes back to its normal state, like a spell broken. Aníbal looks at the door.)

CELESTINA *(Sotto)*: Who's that?
ANÍBAL *(Sotto)*: Stay.

(Aníbal climbs down the ladder. Celestina stays up on the bed, partially hidden from view by the downstage footboard.

Aníbal opens the door. Sirens. Aníbal is surprised by the sight of hundreds of Sparkletts water bottles covering the porch.

Nelson is there. Nelson looks different. His hair is slightly longer. His mustache is gone. His army clothes have been replaced by blue jeans, sneakers and an old jean jacket. He walks with a cane.

But that's not the only thing that's changed. Something childlike and happy has been taken away from Nelson. Though he mouths some of the same old lines, they lack his spirit.)

Nelson?
NELSON *(Tired smile)*: Brother!

(Nelson scoops up Aníbal in a bear hug and pounds his back.)

ANÍBAL *(Confused)*: What are you doing here?

(Nelson holds Aníbal for a long time. Aníbal has to pull away. Nelson won't let him.)

NELSON: Look at you! You get older and uglier all the time!
ANÍBAL: Everything okay?
NELSON: Fucking just wanna hold you, man.

(Aníbal, worried, pulls away from Nelson.)

ANÍBAL: What happened? Couldn't you get back to Death Valley? Are the freeways closed?
NELSON: Death *Valley?* What are you talking about? Everything's great. Hey, I'm a free man! I can do whatever I want now!
ANÍBAL *(Noticing)*: Hey, what happened to you? Why's your face like that?

(Nelson comes into the living room, closing the door behind him. Sirens stop. Nelson looks around.)

NELSON: Fuckme, the old place hasn't changed at all. Everything's just the way I remember it!
ANÍBAL: Wait. Wait a minute. What happened to you? You look totally—why are your clothes like that?
NELSON: Jesus, will you get over my *appearance?* What are you, *gay?* I'm lucky to be *alive*, motherfucker. I need a beer.

(Nelson goes to the refrigerator to get a beer.)

ANÍBAL *(Still confused)*: Have a beer.
NELSON: I was pissed at you, bro. I don't mind telling you. All my letters to you came back, your phone's been disconnected, I thought, "That asshole moved without telling me! He makes me drive cross-country—three fucking days—and he's not there, I'mma kill him!"

(Beat.)

ANÍBAL: You've been driving three days?

NELSON: Hello? From *Georgia*? Have you gone *stupid*? You have no *memory*? What did I tell you two years ago? Soon's I get to Benning, get my discharge and my divorce from Mein Kampf, I was comin' back here, find that girl, and ask her to marry me.

(A short beat as Aníbal looks at Nelson.)

ANÍBAL: Two years? Nelson are you drunk? That was only a few minutes ago you left here and said that.

NELSON *(Laughs)*: You gotta get outta L.A., bro. Your *brain*!

ANÍBAL: A half hour—

NELSON: Maybe to *you*! Mr. Lalaland! You still got on the same boring clothes you had that night! And wasn't it raining then?

ANÍBAL *(Nervous, worried)*: Cut the shit, Nelson . . .

NELSON: *You* cut the shit or I'll body slam you! Where's Celestina? You hiding her? Did she have her baby? Does the baby know who I am? Does he ask about me? I bet he loves me!

ANÍBAL *(Trying to focus)*: She . . . she uh . . .

NELSON: And you! You fuck! Why did all my letters come back? You think it was fun being out in fucking Bosnia and not hearing from you all that fucking time!? Fuck you!

ANÍBAL: Bosnia?

NELSON: Yo, the *war*? The Battle of Mostar? Are you stoned or what? Don't they get the news in L.A.? *(Nelson reaches into his raincoat and pulls up a handful of medals. He throws them across the room, one by one.)* R-com with two oak-leaf clusters! Army Achievement Medal! Bronze Star with three oak-leaf clusters! Silver star with two oak-leaf clusters! Bosnia Liberation Medal!

(Nelson laughs and digs into another pocket and pulls out a dozen letters he wrote to Aníbal, all of which were returned to him. Aníbal looks with amazement at their postmarks.)

ANÍBAL: These letters are from Bosnia.

NELSON: Beautiful land. I met a pregnant girl, too. Man, I really wanted to marry her—broke my heart to leave her—but "no," I said, "I have the most beautiful girl named Celestina waiting for me in the States!"

(Aníbal, shaking, puts the letters down.)

ANÍBAL: How can one night be two years . . . Celestina . . . ?

(Celestina sits up in the bed and climbs down the ladder to the living room during the following:)

NELSON: They had to fucking put me in a fucking army hospital 'cause I have a fucking nervous *breakdown?* I thought: I gotta live through this so I can see my bride and my child again! And I said this to myself, Aníbal, over and over, like a prayer, and you know *that was the only thing* that kept some fucking Serbian sniper bullet from finding the back of my head or some land mine from erasing my legs. The unbearable luck of her *name!*

(Celestina is in the living room. Nelson turns to face her. He can't believe what he sees.)

CELESTINA: Hi Nelson.

(A long pause as Nelson just takes her in and smiles.)

NELSON: Hey.

CELESTINA: How are you?

NELSON: That's really you.

CELESTINA: It's really me.

NELSON *(Answering her question)*: I'm a little tired. Ass hurts from driving three days from Georgia!

(Nelson starts to cry. Celestina goes to him.)

CELESTINA: Hey, hey, what is it?

NELSON: Nothing. It's nothing. No problem.

(Celestina wipes Nelson's eyes.)

CELESTINA: I heard what happened to you in the war. I'm really sorry.

NELSON: It's over. I lived. I'm gonna forget it as soon as I can.

CELESTINA *(Touching her stomach)*: I have a lot to tell you . . . as you can see . . .

NELSON: Oh yeah! Uh-huh! I can see a lot has happened in your life, Celestina!

ANÍBAL *(To Celestina)*: Do you know what's going on here?

CELESTINA *(Torn)*: Don't be afraid, Aníbal, please . . .

NELSON *(Not listening)*: But what's weird? I'm looking at you. It's like you never aged a day!

CELESTINA: That's because I haven't!

NELSON: And you're pregnant again. Just like that night!

CELESTINA: It's not—Nelson—that's what I have to tell you—and you know I'd only tell you the truth. You left Los Angeles. You went to war . . . but here, in this house, time didn't pass; it's still the same night; you left a little while ago. And this baby . . . it's Rodrigo's baby . . . do you understand that . . . ?

NELSON *(Laughs)*: Fuck you!

CELESTINA: It's the truth!

NELSON: I can't believe you would lie to me!

CELESTINA: And Aníbal—two years have passed—whether you want to believe it or not!

ANÍBAL: How is that possible?

CELESTINA: It's me, Aníbal. I've infected you! I've changed the "time" around you—

ANÍBAL: But—who's been paying the light bill?! Who's been paying the rent?! Where's Debbie been?! What happened to my job?!

NELSON: What the fuck are you two trying to do to me?!

CELESTINA *(To both men)*: Things have *happened* . . .

NELSON *(Overlapping with Celestina)*: Look, I *know* that's Aníbal's baby! Okay?! I can see what happened!

CELESTINA: Nothing happened!

NELSON: You two fell in love! It's cool! And I guess we didn't make any promises to each other, huh Celestina?

CELESTINA: I'm sorry, Nelson . . .

NELSON: So I just want to see that little baby before I go! Where is he? Where's that little boy I talked to? Did something happen to him?!

CELESTINA: He hasn't been born!

NELSON *(Angry)*: Man, I don't need to hear this double-talk BULLSHIT any more! Fuck you both! I don't give a fuck if you two fell in love with each other! I was stupid to think you would wait for me! But you didn't! *You didn't wait for me, did you!?*

(Nelson makes a move toward Celestina. Aníbal tries to protect her. Nelson grabs Aníbal, lifts him up and body slams him into the floor.

Celestina goes to Aníbal and holds him. Aníbal writhes in pain, speechless. Nelson is breathing hard, instantly sorry he hurt his brother.

Silence.

Nelson quietly cries.)

ANÍBAL *(In pain)*: Oh my God.

NELSON: I'm sorry, bro. I'm not myself. Something in myself got taken out sometime as I was looking through the sights of the tank, lining up targets, watching things blow up. Jesus shit! I got so much I gotta forget!

ANÍBAL: Jesus Christ, bro . . .

(Nelson goes to Aníbal, lifts him and puts him gently on the sofa bed. He holds Aníbal.)

NELSON: I'm sorry, bro, you know I fucking love you, man! I'm a total asshole! I shouldn't have come here! You got something good with your woman, man, that's cool, that's great! I gotta step aside and let your happiness be, man! Fuck me! I'm sorry! You're my fucking brother and I'm sorry!

ANÍBAL: Nelson . . .

(Nelson wipes his eyes and goes to the door. He opens it. Sirens. Nelson runs out into the night.)

Nelson? Nelson!

(Aníbal gets up to follow Nelson.)

CELESTINA: Aníbal—don't leave me alone!

(Aníbal goes to the door.)

ANÍBAL: I gotta talk to him!

(Aníbal runs out into the night to chase down Nelson, closing the door behind him.

Celestina is alone. She goes to the door and waits for Aníbal. She closes the door. She opens it again. She closes it again. She sits.

In moments she has no idea how much time has passed since Aníbal left. For all she knows it could be days, weeks later. She's getting more and more nervous. Nervousness gives way to panic. She shakes. She looks around.

Unable to bear the pain of waiting any longer, Celestina gets quickly dressed. She puts on her shoes and Aníbal's suede jacket. She goes to the door.

Celestina runs out into the night, leaving the door open.

The digital clocks stop blinking and a new time comes on: 8:06.

Aníbal comes in. He's got his arm around Nelson, who is soaking wet and looks disheveled. Aníbal helps Nelson sit. Nelson sits with his face in his hands. Aníbal closes the door behind him. Sirens stop. Aníbal looks very shaken.)

ANÍBAL *(To Nelson)*: . . . it's okay . . . it's okay, bro . . . you're
home . . .
NELSON: Thanks, man.

ANÍBAL: Celestina! I found him! Bet you thought we'd never get back! Took all night but I got him!

(No answer. Aníbal goes to the offstage bathroom.)

Celestina?

(No response. Aníbal goes back to the living room.)

Celestina!
NELSON: Celestina!
ANÍBAL: Goddammit.
NELSON: Where is she?
ANÍBAL: Her shoes are gone . . . the jacket . . . all the clocks are going . . . she's taken off . . . *shit!* . . . stay here . . . *(He grabs a coat and runs out into the rain. From offstage:)* Celestina!

(The door closes with a slam. Nelson is left alone onstage. Lights start to go down on him.)

NELSON: Celestina.

(Lights to black. The sound of the rain stops. Nelson calls out in the dark, silent house.)

Celestina!

(Blackout.)

EPILOGUE

In the dark, the bolero from the Prologue starts again, though quieter, distorted if possible. Lights come up downstage.

During Celestina's speech, the crew comes on and disassembles the house. By the end of Celestina's speech, there should be nothing left of Aníbal's house in Echo Park.

The ladders next to the bed are removed and the bed is lowered to the stage. The glass wall is removed from the house and left freestanding, to the side. Water drips down the side of the glass wall, as in the Prologue. A microphone on a C-stand is placed down center.

It's forty years later.

Celestina enters and goes to the microphone. She's no longer pregnant. Her clothes are nicer than before. But otherwise she looks the same. She's pushing a stroller. She wears Aníbal's aged suede jacket. She's talking to the baby. She's in mid-conversation.

CELESTINA: Can you believe this rain for L.A.? *Coño! (Beat)* The last time I was here it was raining just like this, right before you were born, and Los Angeles has changed so much, *mijo.* I can't get over it. The Big One was finally born—a monster with seven epicenters—releasing unimaginable waves of energy and killing many unprepared people—the six active oil fields on Pico exploded—glass came down from the towers in

Downtown and Century City and Burbank like floating guillotines—there were fourteen million refugees—and Los Angeles died for a while. People went back to New York and the Midwest. There was a long sleep. *(Beat)*

But people came back. They came back for the things they loved about L.A. the first time. They rebuilt the city. And the city was reborn—and now it's better than ever! Look, *mijo*, you see? That building over there? That's the White House. They moved it from Washington, D.C., and put it on Wilshire Boulevard. And there's the United Nations building and the World Trade Center. All of it is here in the new L.A. The new capital of the United States. The capital of world culture and trade. The capital of the Third World. Boy, they really fixed this place up, Aníbal! The largest subway system in the world is here, connecting everything from Catalina Island to the Angeles National Forest. The air is clean! It's chic to read! All the street signs are in Spanish! They integrated all the neighborhoods! There are no more poor sections! No more big earthquakes for another one hundred and fifty years! In L.A., that's forever!

(The house has been completely dismantled and removed from the stage. It looks like the opening of the play. The bolero ends or fades out.

In the dark, Aníbal enters and lies on the bed.

Celestina pushes the stroller to the bed.

Lights on the bed go up. We can see clearly that Aníbal is an old man in his seventies. Aníbal lies in bed, reading a book.

The light around the bed goes very dark, leaving the bed in limbo. The vague twinkling stars, crescent moons and dark, silvery clouds of the earlier scene could return: it should seem as if once again the bed were floating in space.

Celestina goes to Aníbal's side and she looks at him a long moment.)

CELESTINA *(Big smile)*: Is that really you, Aníbal?
ANÍBAL *(Looking up from his book)*: Huh?
CELESTINA: It's me, Aníbal! I'm back! I just got into L.A.! I didn't

think I'd remember how to get to Echo Park—but that bus stop at Virgil and Santa Monica is still there—and your house is exactly the same—the earthquake didn't hurt it—I can't believe my luck!

(Aníbal looks at Celestina a long moment. He doesn't remember her.)

ANÍBAL: Are you the new nurse?
CELESTINA: It's me. It's Celestina! I'm back!
ANÍBAL: You're not the new nurse? Who's going to give me a bath?
CELESTINA: . . . I'm Celestina.
ANÍBAL: Who is Celestina?
CELESTINA: Aníbal, stop it.
ANÍBAL: Who are you?

(Beat.)

CELESTINA: Celestina del Sol.

(Celestina waits for the name to click in Aníbal's memory. It doesn't. Aníbal holds out his hand.)

ANÍBAL: I'm Aníbal de la Luna. Nice to meet you.

(Disappointed, Celestina shakes hands with Aníbal.)

CELESTINA: Nice to meet you.
ANÍBAL: Are you here for the house? It's a craftsman. Built in the last century. In the forties.
CELESTINA: Don't you remember me at all?
ANÍBAL: When did we meet?
CELESTINA: I think it was forty years ago, but I can't be sure.
ANÍBAL: Forty years! *Coño!* Memory doesn't go back that far!
CELESTINA: It's just like yesterday for me! You picked me up by the side of the road. I was pregnant. You took me to this house. We had quesadillas! You rubbed my feet!
ANÍBAL: I did?

CELESTINA: I remember every moment of that night! I never stopped thinking about you! And I meant to come back sooner, but I just lost track of the "time"!

ANÍBAL: It couldn't have been forty years ago. Eyesight isn't so hot—these damn cataracts, you know?—but—you're a kid. What're you, twenty-five? Twenty-six?

(Slight beat.)

CELESTINA: I'm not really sure.

(This response seems to jog something in Aníbal's memory, but he isn't sure what.)

ANÍBAL: Well, if you're here for the house, make yourself at home, look around—it's a craftsman!

CELESTINA: I know it's a fucking craftsman, Aníbal!

ANÍBAL *(Laughs; re: baby)*: And who's that little guy?

CELESTINA: My son. I think I was in labor with him for six months!

ANÍBAL: Again, please?

CELESTINA: Never mind!

ANÍBAL: How old is he?

CELESTINA: Do you think I know?

ANÍBAL: Why do I feel like I've had this conversation before?

CELESTINA: His name is Aníbal. Aníbal del Sol y la Luna. His father's dead. Rodrigo's body was pulled out of the L.A. River in the storm of the century.

ANÍBAL: *Coño!*

CELESTINA: It was the night that we met, Aníbal. Your brother was in the army. You had a girlfriend named Debbie.

ANÍBAL: Debbie? You're a week too late. We buried her last week in Anaheim. Disney did a fucking hell of a job burying my wife, let me tell you. Those people know how to throw a funeral! They are true merchants of death!

CELESTINA: So you married her, huh?

ANÍBAL: Had to. Knocked her up.

CELESTINA: And Nelson?

ANÍBAL: He's a war hero, you know. Lives up the street. Married a beautiful girl many years ago . . . a Bosnian. They have thirteen kids!

CELESTINA *(Smiles)*: Good.

(Aníbal stares at Celestina a long moment.)

ANÍBAL: You look . . . *coño* . . . you look so familiar. You look vaguely like . . . there was a young woman . . . on a night that seemed to last forever . . . she was . . . crazy . . . and very fat . . .

CELESTINA: I was pregnant!

ANÍBAL: . . . but it was some forty years ago . . . before the Big One . . . before they moved the capital . . . something happened to me back then . . . I blacked out for a couple of years . . . nobody could explain it . . . I woke up and it was two years later! I had dreams in my coma that made no sense! *(Laughs)* But you know what? It was so long ago and so much has happened since then, so much life, so much dying, so many changes, it just gets buried under all the time between now and then, you know? It's like, somewhere in my mind is a ditch, a very dark and deep hole, and time keeps filling this hole with all the debris of my life, the *details*: every name, face, taste, sound: gone! Down the hole! Outta reach! *Coño!* What's the point of that, huh? Does that make any sense to you?

CELESTINA: No.

ANÍBAL: No. You're very beautiful, though. Kind. It would be nice to remember you. To have been in love with you.

CELESTINA: We were in love, Aníbal.

ANÍBAL: How do you know we were in love?

CELESTINA: We lived together for two years, didn't we?

ANÍBAL: We did?

CELESTINA: They were the happiest two years of my life.

ANÍBAL: You sure it was me?

(Beat. Celestina wipes her tears, then reaches out, touches his hand and kisses it.)

CELESTINA: I should probably let you get some sleep. It's been great seeing you again, Aníbal.

ANÍBAL: Yes.

CELESTINA: You take care of yourself, okay?

ANÍBAL: Thanks for dropping by. Listen, this house is a steal at this price! Great place to raise a family!

CELESTINA: I'll keep that in mind.

ANÍBAL: Yes. Good.

CELESTINA: Is there anything I can do for you before I go?

(Beat.)

ANÍBAL: Yes there is.

CELESTINA: What?

ANÍBAL: Would you rub my feet? They're freezing.

(Beat.)

CELESTINA *(Smiles)*: Okay.

(Celestina gets into bed with Aníbal. He puts his feet up on her lap. She rubs his feet gently. The feeling of her hands on his feet has an instant and electrifying effect on Aníbal. When he talks, he sounds like a young man again.)

ANÍBAL: I searched Los Angeles for days and days after she left me. I went to that bus stop on the corner of Virgil and Santa Monica and waited there day and night. I called every hospital and went to every police station in L.A. County. *(Beat)* I imagined finding her. Living with her forever. I imagined long moments of silence between us when we didn't have anything to say. I imagined enduring the terror of a Los Angeles gone out of control because these quiet moments would be like iron wings and we'd be sheltered inside them. We wouldn't hear the noise of the earthquakes or the screams of a dying culture. But she never came back to me. I never saw her again. All I kept were memories of that extraordinary woman and a night that had that dream feeling to it, you know that feeling: there's a sound like suspended music, air that doesn't move, time that doesn't add to itself. It took me years but I finally understood that I had encountered a true mystery that night, that I had taken a living miracle into my house. That Celestina del Sol was from a world I would never understand. That sometimes Nature improvises. That Nature created a woman that lived outside the field of time and may never die. That someday everyone who ever knew her and remembered her would be gone. That she would live forever in that physical perfection like some kind of exiled and forgotten goddess. And that trying to understand such a life, and why love matters to it, why a god would need to be loved too, was like trying to understand the anatomy of the wind or the architecture of silence or cloud tectonics. *(He laughs)* Yeah. What better way to respond to a miracle than to fall in love with it?

(During the following, lights start to go down on the bed. The sound of the rain comes up.)

And at one point in the evening, I heard the sound of Spanish, as love assumed the language my parents spoke the night I was conceived, the language I had forgotten . . .

(Celestina kisses Aníbal. She leaves the bed, takes the baby out of the stroller and starts walking to the bus stop with the baby in her arms.)

Celestina said to me: *"Me pregunto como será haberte amado en cada etapa de tu vida, Aníbal . . . "*

(Aníbal continues the speech in Spanish, quietly, underneath Celestina's simultaneous, and louder, translation:)

CELESTINA *(To the baby):* . . . I wonder what it would be like to love you in every age of your life, Aníbal. To love the little boy you were, and hold your hand, and lead you across the street, and kiss your fat little baby stomach, and comb your little boy's hair. And then, later, to love the old man you've become, and kiss your deep wrinkles, and smooth out the gray hair, and delight your wise and tired heart, and stare into those mysterious eyes, past the cataracts, and deep into you, to the green landscapes where you never age. Wouldn't it be sweet to have that kind of love, Aníbal?

ANÍBAL: *". . . El amor de toda una vida."*

(Celestina has reached the bus stop with the baby.)

CELESTINA: . . . The love of a lifetime.

(Aníbal smiles sadly at the sweet memory. Then he forgets it again and goes back to his book as if nothing happened.

Lights slowly to black on the bed.

At the dark bus stop, Celestina holds her thumb up, hoping to catch a ride out of Los Angeles. She reaches into a pocket and pulls out saltine crackers. She gives one to the baby and eats the other.

Rain. Headlights. Blackout.)